GRAY
MATTER

Sensation and Perception

GRAY
MATTER

GRAY
MATTER

Sensation and Perception

Mike May

Series Editor
Eric H. Chudler, Ph.D.

CHELSEA HOUSE
PUBLISHERS
An imprint of Infobase Publishing

Sensation and Perception

Copyright © 2007 by Infobase Publishing

Chelsea House
An imprint of Infobase Publishing
132 West 31st Street
New York NY 10001

ISBN-10: 0-7910-8958-4
ISBN-13: 978-0-7910-8958-3

Library of Congress Cataloging-in-Publication Data
May, Mike.
  Sensation and perception / Mike May.
      p. cm. — (Gray matter)
  Includes bibliographical references and index.
  ISBN 0-7910-8958-4 (hardcover)
  1. Senses and sensation. 2. Perception. I. Title.
  QP431.M39 2007
  612.8—dc22   2006038552

Chelsea House books are available at special discounts when purchased in bulk quantities for businesses, associations, institutions, or sales promotions. Please call our Special Sales Department in New York at (212) 967-8800 or (800) 322-8755.

You can find Chelsea House on the World Wide Web at http://www.chelseahouse.com

Text and cover design by Terry Mallon

Printed in the United States of America

Bang EJB 10 9 8 7 6 5 4 3 2 1

This book is printed on acid-free paper.

All links and Web addresses were checked and verified to be correct at the time of publication. Because of the dynamic nature of the Web, some addresses and links may have changed since publication and may no longer be valid.

Contents

1 The Basics of Sensation and Perception

Find two quarters and grasp one by its edges with your left thumb and forefinger. Hold the other coin the same way with your right hand. Hold the left coin about a foot away from your eyes, so that you can see George Washington's head, and hold the right coin at arm's length. Although one quarter is much closer to your eyes, they both look about the same size. Now, close your right eye. Suddenly, the right quarter looks noticeably smaller than the left one. You just demonstrated two basic principles of science: observation and experimentation. You observed the quarters, then changed the conditions and looked at them again. What you observe and how you interpret it lies at the very heart of **sensation** and **perception**.

Some groundwork must be considered before the optical illusion with the quarters is explained. A sensation arises from something in the environment that impacts the bodily systems that gather surrounding information, including tasting, hearing, seeing, smelling, and touching. We also feel things from inside, such as a hungry, rumbling stomach. We have specialized structures—such as the eye—that collect this information. How you actually "see," though, depends on perception, the conscious experience of what you sense. In the quarter illusion described above, you perceive the quarters as the same size at first, and then as different sizes.

Working together, sensation and perception provide the crucial capability to survive. Without sensation and perception, for instance, we'd never consider steering clear of a bear or dodging a speeding car.

To understand this field of science, many scientists think of a series of steps that make up the process of perception (Figure 1.1). This process consists of six basic steps: environmental stimulus, **transduction**, processing, perception, recognition, and action. The environmental stimulus is anything around us that we can possibly perceive, such as light or sound. Transduction converts energy in the environment, such as light, to some form of information inside us, such as an electrical or chemical signal. Combining the environmental stimulus with transduction generates a sensation. Then that sensation is processed, usually in the brain. Perception is next, which involves you trying to figure out the sensation. The stages of processing and perception also depend on knowledge. For instance, if you touch a stapler with your eyes closed, you probably recognize it as a stapler because of past knowledge. If you have never seen or even heard of a stapler, you might perceive it very differently, say, as just an odd-shaped piece of metal. That is also part of recognition—giving some meaning to a sensation, such as knowing that a stapler is used to drive a staple through sheets of paper.

Many perceptions, although not all, lead to the last step in the perceptual process—action, or doing something because of a stimulus. For example, if you come across a bear while hiking, the perceptual process leads to action: slowly moving away, preferably undetected by the bear. Then a new set of sensations feeds into the perceptual process as you continue on your hike.

HOW RECEPTORS WORK

To make the perceptual process work, humans and other animals possess **receptors** to capture different kinds of energy from

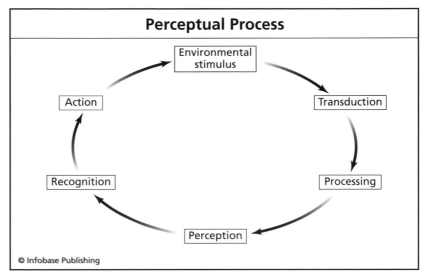

Figure 1.1 The perceptual process describes the reaction to an environmental stimulus. We decode the information and eventually act on it. The action impacts the next environmental stimulus.

the environment. For example, cells in the eye's **retina** capture light and change the light energy into electrical energy. The transduction of a stimulus depends on nerve cells (**neurons**). Neurons function through the entire perceptual process. This process starts at the receptors, gets processed in the brain, and sends out signals that make a person do something in response to the stimulus.

Neurons make up the basic units in the brain. Their function is to collect and transmit information. The structure of a neuron includes four main parts: **dendrites, soma** (cell body), **axon**, and **nerve terminals** (Figure 1.2). The neuron's branchlike dendrites are connected to the soma. The axon extends like a telephone wire from the soma. The end of an axon usually has small protrusions, called nerve terminals. Information commonly enters a neuron through the dendrites, gets processed in the soma, and is sent down the axon to the nerve terminals, where it is then

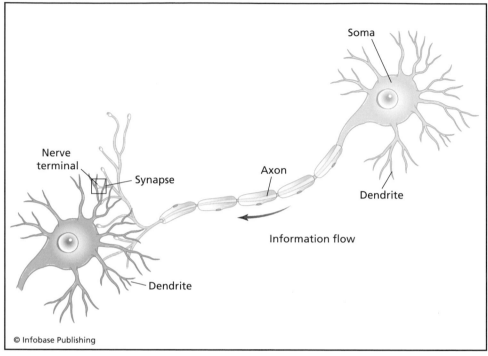

Figure 1.2 A neuron's basic anatomy consists of four parts: a soma, dendrites, an axon, and nerve terminals. Information is received by dendrites, gets collected in the cell body, and flows down the axon.

passed to the dendrites of another neuron. The location where an axon terminal meets a receiving neuron—either on a dendrite or directly on the soma—is known as a **synapse** (Figure 1.3).

The flow of information along a chain of neurons moves in electric waves called **action potentials** (Figure 1.4). These waves can travel very fast. In some cat neurons, for example, scientists have clocked action potentials at 268 miles per hour (432 kilometers per hour).[1] For comparison, race car driver Eddie Cheever drove the fastest lap ever during the Indianapolis 500 race in 1996. His average speed was 236.10 miles per hour (379.97 km/h). Action potentials in some neurons would have outpaced Cheever.

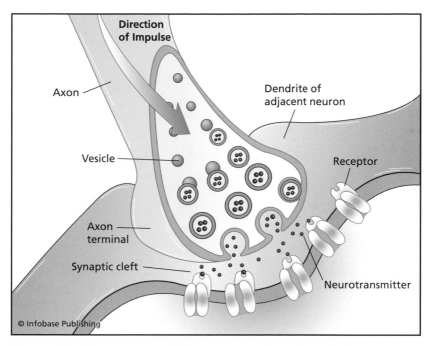

Figure 1.3 Neurons connect at synapses, where chemical messengers known as neurotransmitters travel from one neuron to another.

The fluid inside neurons consists of water and dissolved **ions**, which are atoms with an electrical charge. These charged atoms can move in and out of a neuron through **ion channels**— microscopic pores in a neuron. Different amounts of positive and negative ions inside and outside of a neuron act like little batteries, which make the inside of a neuron a bit more negatively charged than the outside. If many ion channels open, they can create a wave of electric energy, or action potential, that runs down an axon. The action potential carries information from the soma to the nerve terminals. Because an action potential moves so fast, a neuron can fire (set off an action potential) time after time if it keeps getting stimulated. In some cases, a neuron can fire hundreds of times in a second.[2]

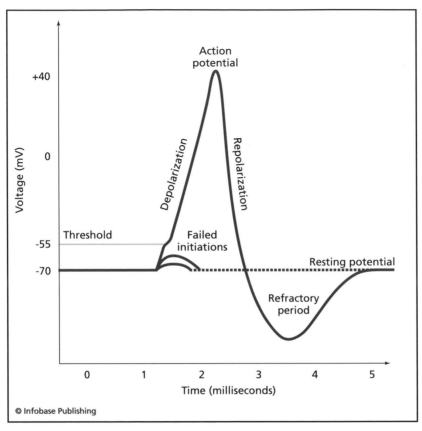

Figure 1.4 Action potentials carry information along nerves. When a neuron is not active, the electrical charge is more negative inside the cell than outside it. Turning the cell on causes positively charged atoms to move into the cell, which depolarizes the cell, or makes the inside positive. The electrical wave peaks and then repolarizes, or goes back to a negative inside charge. During the refractory period, the neuron cannot fire again.

What causes the ion channels to open? A firing neuron (one making action potentials) releases chemicals called **neurotransmitters** from the nerve terminals. The neurotransmitters drift across the little space between one neuron and the next (known as the synaptic cleft) and then attach to a receptor on the dendrite of a receiving neuron. A neurotransmitter fits into a receptor much like a key fits into a lock. When the two combine, ion channels open or close. If enough of the right channels get affected, an action potential will be triggered in the receiving neuron and the information will continue along the chain.

In 1921, Austrian scientist Otto Loewi discovered the first neurotransmitter—acetylcholine—in the heart of a frog. This neurotransmitter causes voluntary muscles, such as a bicep, to contract. When a person squeezes his hand to hold a glass, acetylcholine causes his muscles to contract. This same chemical also carries messages between neurons in many parts of the brain.

Chemical messages between neurons can make the receiving neuron either more or less likely to turn on. When neurotransmitters bind to some receptors on a neuron, it is more likely to fire, or be excited. On the other hand, attachment to other receptors makes a neuron less likely to fire; it is inhibited. People often think of making something work by turning it on. In the brain, there's just as much value in being able to turn off a system as there is in turning one on. For example, imagine if you could not turn off, or block out, some ongoing stimuli, such as an annoying buzz from a furnace. By being able to tune out the buzz, you can focus your attention on more important stimuli, such as the words you read in a book.

A nerve's axon can carry information a long way. Some axons are microscopic in length, and some are more than 3 feet (1 meter) long. Some axons are coated with **myelin**, a fatty substance that provides insulation to help action potentials travel quickly. Myelin is similar to the plastic coating on electrical wires.

THE VALUE OF NETWORKS

With electrical and chemical signals flowing all over in the nervous system, how does it decode the information that it gathers? How does the nervous system know the difference between a flash of light and a clap of thunder? In 1842, German scientist Johannes Mueller came up with a possible answer. He called it the doctrine of specific nerve energies. Mueller's theory suggested that what we perceive depends on which neurons get

Introducing the Brain

In the fourth century B.C., a Greek philosopher and scientist named Aristotle believed that the human heart contained the mind. As we now know, it doesn't. Instead, the mind resides in roughly 3 pounds (1.4 kg) of fatty tissue in our head, the brain. No one knows exactly how many neurons make up our brain, but estimates range from 10 billion to 1 trillion.[3] Even at the low end of that estimate, this means that one human brain has about twice as many neurons as there are people on Earth.

The brain is made up of many different parts, but the section that is of most interest to the subject of this book is the cerebral cortex. The cerebral cortex consists of four sections, or lobes: the frontal, occipital, parietal, and temporal (Figure 1.5). In general, different areas of the brain perform different tasks. For example, visual processing takes place in the occipital lobe. The processing of information related to touch takes place in the parietal lobe. Some scientists have further divided the cortex into specific areas that perform particular functions. Increasing technological abilities, however, have shown researchers that many processes in the brain are widely distributed in different areas.

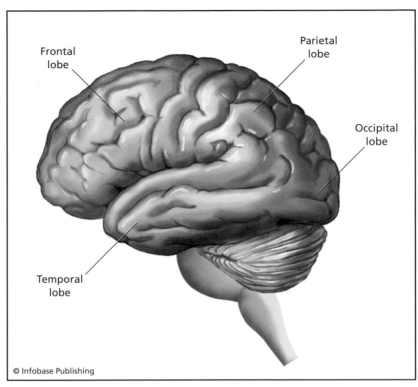

Frontal lobe

Parietal lobe

Occipital lobe

Temporal lobe

© Infobase Publishing

Figure 1.5 Scientists label the cerebral cortex of the human brain as four main lobes: frontal, occipital, parietal, and temporal.

activated. If it's neurons in your eyes, you see. Activation of neurons in your ears makes you hear.

But really, it's not quite that easy. Your eyes and your ears capture a wide variety of information from the environment. Then collections of thousands—maybe even millions—of neurons work together to sort out what kind of information a receptor grabbed from the environment. That job gets even more difficult because the nervous system must unravel the data fast, sometimes extremely fast. If you are walking across a street and a car swerves around a corner and heads right toward you, your brain must quickly analyze the situation. How fast is it going? Can you get out of the way? How should you get away? Your brain needs to complete the perceptual process with the right action—and all as fast as possible, the kind of speed that might save your life.

■ **Learn more about the contents of this chapter** Search the Internet for *sensation*, *perception*, and *action potential*.

2 | Visual Sensation

It was 1958, and scientists knew rather little about how the brain processed visual information. But at the Johns Hopkins School of Medicine in Baltimore, Maryland, Dr. Torsten Wiesel and Dr. David Hubel monitored the electrical activity of a live cat's cerebral cortex while showing the animal different images. The researchers recorded the activity of a single neuron for hours. A sound speaker amplified the electrical signal of the neuron so they could actually hear the neuron's activity.

Hubel and Wiesel also used a device that could project a light or dark spot into the cat's eyes. This was similar to an old-fashioned slide projector. To get a light spot, they loaded the device with a brass slide with a little hole drilled in it; to get a dark spot, they used a glass slide with a little black dot on it. Then they shone a light through the device. Every now and then, the neuron in the cat's brain would fire action potentials, but it would fire even when there was no spot aimed at the cat's eyes. It seemed like something Hubel and Wiesel were doing was making the action potentials fire. But they couldn't figure out what specific stimulus was causing this reaction. Was it the white spot? The black one? Was it something else entirely?

Eventually, the two scientists realized what consistently turned on the neuron: a shadow moved across the cat's eyes each time Hubel and Wiesel changed the slide. The neurons did not react to the image of the slide in general. Also, these neurons did not respond to spots of light on the slide, as other neurons in the visual cortex might do. Instead, these neurons looked for edges. The spot- and edge-reacting neurons show that the visual cortex can examine an image in pieces—for example, the spots or edges that make up parts of an image. Later in processing, the brain puts bits of information together to get a complete picture. Hubel and Wiesel's experiment turned out to be part of the work that earned them the 1981 Nobel Prize in Physiology or Medicine.

THE PHYSICS OF LIGHT

Being able to understand how humans see begins with an understanding of what exactly is light. Light is made of particles called **photons.** At the same time, light is also made of waves. The waves of light come from what is called the **electromagnetic spectrum** (Figure 2.1)—waves of electricity and magnetism that can move through air and water. This spectrum runs from very long waves—such as radio waves—to incredibly short ones—such as X-rays. For humans, the part of the spectrum that matters for vision is called visible light, and it lies more or less in the middle of the electromagnetic spectrum.

You have likely seen a wave in the ocean, either in person or when looking at a photograph. The shape of a wave starts low, rises forward in a curve, and then returns to the original low spot. If we could freeze a wave in place, get out a ruler, and measure from one low spot to the next, or from one peak to the next peak, we would find the **wavelength.** The wavelength of visible light, however, is much too small to measure with a ruler. Visible light comes in wavelengths that range from 400 to 700 **nanometers.** A nanometer is one-billionth of a meter. A

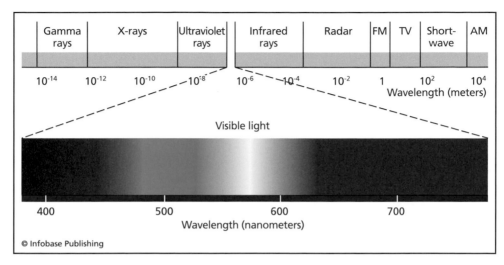

Figure 2.1 The electromagnetic spectrum consists of all the waves that travel around us, including X-rays and radio waves. It also includes the visible spectrum, which is light that humans can see.

nanometer is so small that it takes almost 18 million nanometers to equal the width of a dime.

The wavelength of visible light also helps determine the color of the light. The spectrum flows smoothly from one color to the next: red, orange, yellow, green, blue, indigo, and violet. The reds come from light with longer wavelengths, and blues come from shorter-wavelength light. The rest fall in between.

ANATOMY OF THE VISUAL SYSTEM

Overall, the sense of sight depends on three main structures: the **eye**, the **lateral geniculate nucleus**, and the **visual cortex** (Figure 2.2). The lateral geniculate nucleus is located in the middle of the brain, and the visual cortex is at the back of the cerebral cortex, in the occipital lobe. This area of the occipital lobe is called the striated cortex, because the nerve cells in it make it look striped. There are many other areas of the brain involved with vision, so, although the visual cortex is one of the first areas for

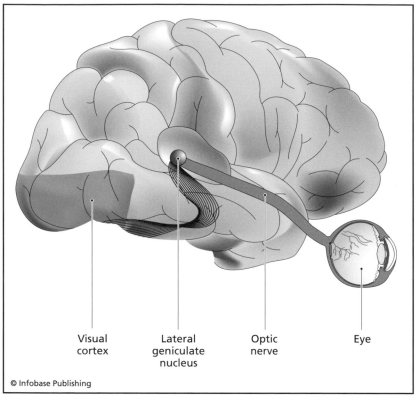

Visual   Lateral   Optic   Eye
cortex   geniculate   nerve
            nucleus

© Infobase Publishing

Figure 2.2 The visual system consists of the eye, which captures light information and sends it to the lateral geniculate nucleus, which then passes the information to the visual cortex.

visual action, it is just part of a very complex collection of areas responsible for sight.

Vision starts at the eye itself. The eye works much like a television camera with many automatic features: It automatically tracks things of interest and it automatically adjusts for focus and light. It even includes an automatic lens-cleaning system. Further up in the brain, the images from a person's two eyes are combined into one. It is a very complex system, providing a daunting challenge to the world's best scientists.

Some of the most interesting action takes place inside the eye's retina, a thin sheet of cells about one-quarter of a millimeter thick that lies at the back of the eye. The retina has light receptors—called **rods** and **cones**—that translate light energy into electrical signals. Rods are long and slender in shape, and cones are cone-shaped. These light receptors are located at the back of the retina, so light must travel through other cells before it reaches the ones that sense the light.

An image can only be seen clearly when light is focused on the retina. If the eye does not focus light on the retina, the image looks blurry, like a photograph that is out of focus. To create a focused image, the eye must bend the waves of light. The closer something is, the more the light must be bent to focus it on the retina. That bending comes from two sources: the **cornea** and the **lens** (Figure 2.3). The cornea is a transparent covering at the very front of the eye, and it does most of the light bending. The lens, which sits inside the eye, is shaped sort of like a ball that is squished in its center. The lens is rubbery and can change shape to help bend the light more or less. Also, the lens turns an image upside down. During processing in the brain, the image is flipped back to its correct orientation.

GETTING AN IMAGE OUT OF THE RETINA

The visual receptors in the retina play different roles. The 120 million rods in each retina sense dim light. The cones—there are about 5 million to 6 million per retina—are used to translate fine detail and color vision. Rods and cones contain **photopigment**, a kind of molecule that can absorb light. A photopigment can grab just one photon of light, the smallest particle of light there is. The energy of photons changes the photopigment's chemical structure, which generates an electrical signal in the visual receptor cell. The chemical process used to detect light depends on a compound made from Vitamin A.

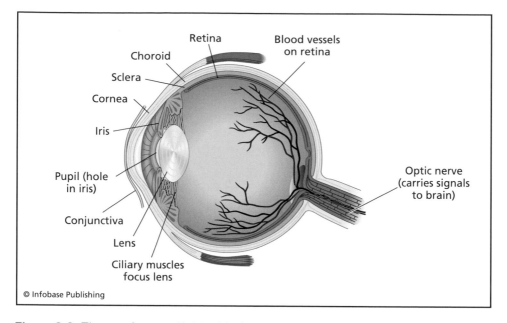

Choroid
Retina
Blood vessels
on retina
Sclera
Cornea
Iris
Pupil (hole
in iris)
Optic nerve
(carries signals
to brain)
Conjunctiva
Lens
Ciliary muscles
focus lens

© Infobase Publishing

Figure 2.3 The eye focuses light with the cornea and lens to deliver a sharp image to the retina. In the retina, photoreceptors convert the light stimulus into electrical signals that are sent to the lateral geniculate nucleus by way of the optic nerve.

Different photopigments are sensitive to light of different wavelengths. Rods, for example, have just one kind of photopigment, so they "see" in black and white. Cones, on the other hand, come in three different varieties based on the photopigment that they contain: blue, green, or red. Rods and cones are not spread evenly over the retina. There are more rods around the edges of the retina, and more cones in the center. The most sensitive part of the retina, called the **macula**, contains many more cones than rods. It is roughly at the center of the retina.

Figure 2.4 (*right*) Light enters the front of the retina, and gets captured at the back of it by rods and cones. Then, the light information moves back toward the front of the retina. Electrical signals move through bipolar cells that connect to the ganglion cells, which make up the optic nerve.

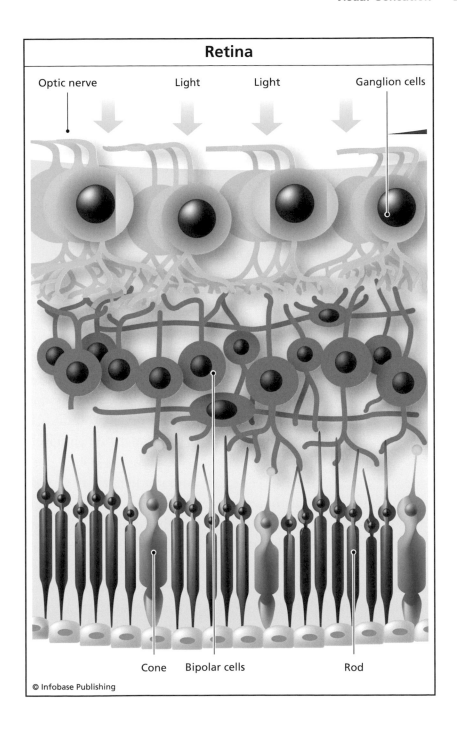

Retina

Optic nerve   Light   Light   Ganglion cells

Cone   Bipolar cells   Rod

© Infobase Publishing

When a person looks directly at something, the visual system lines up the image on the macula.

After light hits the retina and turns on some photoreceptors, the neural signal gets passed from the back of the retina to the front, passing through several layers of cells (Figure 2.4). At the front of the retina, the signal reaches **ganglion cells**. Each retina contains about one million ganglion cells that are gathered up in a bundle at the **optic disk**.

By the time visual signals reach the ganglion cells, the image is already getting processed. Scientists examine this process in part by finding a cell's **receptive field**, which is the location on the retina where light "turns on" the cell. For so-called on-center cells, light at the center of the receptive field turns on the ganglion cell. But light that hits a doughnut-shaped area around the center will turn off the ganglion cell. Off-center cells perform just the opposite: turning off when light hits the receptive field's center, and turning on when light hits the area surrounding the center. Neighboring ganglion cells possess similar receptive fields. That is, neighboring ganglion cells respond to light that hits the retina in similar places. So if one ganglion cell, for example, reacts to light that reaches the upper part of the retina closest to the nose, an adjacent ganglion cell will react to light in about the same area of the retina. As a group, the ganglion cells map the visual field of the retina. In addition, the ganglion cells with the smallest receptive fields react to light that lands on the center of the retina where images are seen in the sharpest focus.

The receptive fields of ganglion cells also demonstrate a common principle of the nervous system: **lateral inhibition**. This is the idea that cells that lie close to one another can turn each other off. Imagine a sheet of retina with photoreceptors all over it. Then, draw a doughnut shape on the retina's surface. The visual cells inside the doughnut's hole make up the center, and those on the ring of the doughnut make up the surrounding cells. If this doughnut and hole makes up the receptive field of an on-center ganglion cell, light hitting the photoreceptors in the center turns on the ganglion cell, and light hitting the visual receptors in the surrounding ring turns off the ganglion cell. So putting equal amounts of light in the center and the surrounding ring cancels the output from the ganglion cell. The cells in the center and those in the surrounding ring inhibit each other.

This leads to some odd perceptions. A commonly used example of lateral inhibition in vision is a set of squares, where there's a white square and a black one and each has a smaller gray square in the middle (Figure 2.5). In comparison, the gray square inside the white square seems darker than the gray square inside the black square. Or rather, it seems quite obvious until you cut out the two gray squares and look at them side by side. They are actually the same color.

How could this show lateral inhibition? Think about a place where the inside edge of the white square touches the gray square. The white turns on the photoreceptors that it hits. At the same time, those photoreceptors might turn off nearby cells that see the gray square, which would make it seem darker. On the other hand, where the black square touches the gray square, the surrounding photoreceptors that get hit by the black do not get turned on much and add little inhibition to the cells that see the gray square; in that case, the gray seems lighter.

This example also reveals a common feature of sensory systems. Instead of picking up an absolute quantity—such as the true physical intensity of light coming from the gray areas—the nervous system often records variation. It is difference that our sensory system often focuses on most carefully.

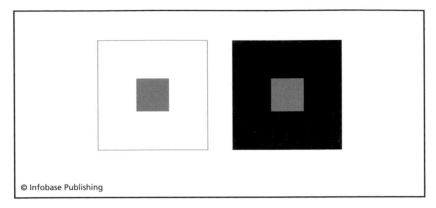

© Infobase Publishing

Figure 2.5 An experiment showing lateral inhibition. The gray square on the left looks darker than the gray square on the right, but in reality they are the same shade of gray.

GETTING IMAGES TO THE BRAIN

The information from the retina—carried in the roughly one million ganglion cells from each eye—gathers in the optic nerve. This nerve bundle leaves the back of the eye at a place called the optic disk. There is no room for photoreceptors at the optic disk, creating what is known as a "blind spot." The optic nerve carries almost 40% of all nerve fibers that enter the brain.[4] That is especially amazing if one considers that the four other senses—hearing, smell, taste, and touch—must also send nerves to the brain, and all sorts of muscle and joint sensors send nerves too. Nevertheless, the many lines of information dedicated to the eye reveal how much visual data the brain must capture to process what our eyes detect.

Soon after leaving the eyes, the two optic nerves cross at the optic chiasm. At this location, information that a person sees with his right eye travels to the left side of the brain for processing, and what he sees with his left eye goes to the right side of the brain. Although visual information crosses at the optic chiasm, some of the ganglion cells from both eyes go to both sides of the brain. The side of the right eye's retina closest to the nose and the side of the left eye's retina closest to the ear both record visual information coming from the right. These ganglion cells go to the left side of the brain. The nose side of the left eye's retina and the ear side of the right eye's retina both record visual information coming from the left. These ganglion cells go to the right side of the brain.

Visual information goes to many places in the cortex. In fact, no one knows for sure how many parts of the brain really contribute to vision. The first place the information reaches is the lateral geniculate nucleus, deep inside the brain in the **thalamus**, and then the cerebral cortex—essentially the outer layer of the brain. Place your right hand over the back of your head with your thumb tucked under the bump at the base of your skull, and your hand will cover the visual cortex. This

The Best Vision in the Animal World

Visual acuity describes how well an animal sees details. Among humans, 20/20 is considered to be normal vision. It simply means that someone can see details from 20 feet away as well as someone with normal vision can see the same details from the same distance. People with 20/60 vision need to be within 20 feet of an object to see it as well as a person with normal vision could see it at 60 feet.

Some of the best visual acuity in the world comes from birds. In fact, most birds of prey see much better than humans do. The visual acuity of falcons, for example, is 2.6 times better than that of humans.[5] Falcons can see an object as small as 4 inches (10 cm) wide from a distance of nearly one mile (1.5 km). That's like a person spotting a dime from three football fields away.

area consists of many parts. The one most often discussed is the primary visual cortex, which gets direct input from the lateral geniculate nucleus.

HOW CORTICAL CELLS PROCESS IMAGES

To unravel how animals interpret what they see, scientists spend long hours recording the responses of visual cells to different images. As already mentioned, ganglion cells start to process visual information with center-surround receptive fields. Similar fields exist in cells in the lateral geniculate nucleus. In the primary visual cortex, though, things start to change. If a scientist examines a cell in an animal's primary visual cortex while shining light on the animal's retina, the cell may show no response at all. Those cells need more specific stimuli.

Hubel and Wiesel's research helps explain how those cortical cells respond. The two men found several distinct kinds of cells in the primary visual cortex. The simplest one is called—not surprisingly—a simple cell. Somewhat like ganglion cells, these cells have areas where light turns them on and other areas where light turns them off. Instead of circular receptive fields, though, these cells tend to have rectangular receptive fields. For example, a simple cell can have a receptive field that looks like a three-layer cake, where light on the top and bottom layers turns off the cell, and light on the middle layer turns it on. There are other arrangements for these receptive fields, but they are all made up of rectangular areas.

Also, the receptive fields for simple cells get smaller for parts of the visual field where a person focuses. So, a cortical cell that records information in the periphery usually has a larger receptive field than a cell that concentrates on things directly ahead. In addition, most processing power is given where details are likely to matter the most. Important information can come from anywhere—directly ahead, off-center, or from the periphery. Anyone who has ever played dodgeball knows the value of good peripheral vision.

In Hubel and Wiesel's work, the cat neuron that responded to a moving edge is called a complex cell. An experiment that records cells in the primary visual cortex will most likely find

The Blind Spot

A simple experiment can reveal the retina's blind spot, the place where the optic nerve heads to the brain. Usually, people never notice their blind spot. After all, it isn't as though one walks around seeing a world with a hole in it because of that photoreceptor-free area. Somehow, the brain fills in that space, and the world looks complete.

Close your right eye and with your left eye, focus on the cross in this box (Figure 2.6). Then, move your face closer and closer to the images on the page, all the time focusing on the cross with your open left eye. At some point, the black dot will disappear. At that point, the dot has landed on the blind spot of your left eye. Keep moving closer and closer, and the dot will eventually reappear, just as soon as it gets close enough not to land on the blind spot anymore.

© Infobase Publishing

Figure 2.6 Follow the directions in the text to find your blind spot.

a complex cell, because there are more complex cells than any other cell type. A complex cell's receptive field looks for bars of light or edges between dark and light areas, but it is not divided into "on" and "off" areas like a simple cell's field. Instead, as long as the light hits the complex cell's field, it makes it fire. Other complex cells look for moving lines. If a line of light crosses that complex cell's receptive field, the cell fires. For some of these cells, though, the line must also move in a particular direction.

In addition to dissecting visual information with different sorts of cortical cells, the brain also maps the visual world with a **retinotopic map.** That is, the primary visual cortex resembles a map of the retina in terms of which cells get turned on by light.

■ **Learn more about the contents of this chapter** Search the Internet for *retina, visual cortex,* and *optical illusions.*

3 | Visual Perception

Look at the image of the railroad track (Figure 3.1). Pay special attention to the two rectangles. Which one is bigger? Quite clearly the top rectangle is bigger than the lower one. Now measure the length of the two rectangles. Unbelievable isn't it? They are exactly the same length.

This optical illusion was first described in 1913 by Mario Ponzo, an Italian psychologist. Several hypotheses might explain this illusion, but no one knows precisely why it happens. The most important lesson from the Ponzo illusion, though, is that we do not always perceive things accurately. Instead, we perceive everything in context, or how something appears in relation to things around it.

THE GESTALT OF THINGS

Several scientists who lived during the late 1800s and through the mid-1900s showed that people perceive things a certain way—say, the rectangles in the Ponzo illusion—depending on what else is being perceived at the same time. Max Wertheimer, Wolfgang Köhler, and Kurt Koffka were so-called Gestalt psychologists. The basis of Gestalt psychology is simple: The whole is different than the sum of the parts. In other words, the parts that we sense are combined into something more, once the entire scene is perceived. Several

© Infobase Publishing

Figure 3.1 In the Ponzo illusion, the upper black bar looks longer than the lower one. In reality, they are the same length. Somehow, our perceptual processes make one look bigger than the other.

general principles make up the basis of Gestalt psychology. Some of the concepts that have the most impact on visual perception include proximity, similarity, and good continuation. There are others, too, but examining just these few gives an overall summary of this branch of psychology.

Proximity means that things that are close are connected. In other words, our visual system perceives things that are close together as being connected in some way. For example, in a grid

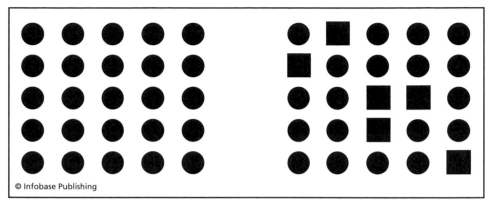

Figure 3.2 In our mind, things that are close together become connected. The dots in the group at the left are closer to each other vertically than horizontally, and we see this collection as columns of dots. Even if the columns include some different symbols, as in the right group, we still see the columns—because of proximity.

of dots, if the dots in columns are closer together than those in the rows, our brain sees the grid as columns of dots (Figure 3.2). On the other hand, if the dots in the rows are closer together than the dots in the columns, we see rows of dots.

Our brain also tends to connect things that look alike. That's the principle of similarity. Consider another grid, but make the first column from dots, the next from stars, the next from dots, and so on. The visual system connects the similar objects and we see a series of columns.

Good continuation means that our brain tends to connect things that show smooth connections instead of sharp turns. If you see two lines that cross, for example, the mind perceives that *X* as being made of two straight lines. The visual system interprets one line going over the other—the smoothest possible explanation. But such an image could also be seen as a line starting at the lower right, angling up to the crossing point, and then turning sharply to the upper right—like a *V* on its side. The other side could be made from another *V* on its side, a mirror image of the *V* on the right side. But that's not how we generally interpret the crossing lines. Instead, our minds believe that images usually continue along smoothly. Keep this in mind, because it's another general feature of perception: Humans tend to perceive things in the environment as they are most likely to be.

ATTENTION AND USING BEST GUESSES

Scientists are certain about one thing regarding vision: The ability to sense and perceive light requires a very complicated brain. To date, scientists know of more than three dozen areas in the brain that contribute to processing vision.[6] This suggests that vision and perception are due to activity in many parts of the brain.

Attention is another thought process that impacts vision. For the most part, we perceive the things that keep our attention. Think of all of the visual information that you never even notice. Things go on in your peripheral vision while you read this book, but since you're focusing on the words on this page, your brain helps you block out those peripheral interruptions. On the other hand, if someone threw a basketball at you while you read, that peripheral motion would likely grab your attention in time to give you a chance to avoid being hit.

Deciding what to pay attention to and what to ignore, depends on experience. For example, people stop responding to things that are continually seen in the peripheral vision. This is referred to as an empirical theory of vision. That means that the visual system learns to perceive things based on what they are most likely to be. If a basketball came into your peripheral vision while you were on a court, you would quickly perceive the object as a basketball. Experience tells you that the most likely round, orange object to enter your vision on a basketball court would be a basketball. It could be a pumpkin, but experience would tell you that would be unlikely. The value of experience applies to all of our senses.

SEEING COLORS

Scientists struggled for centuries to explain color vision. Historically, scientists explained aspects of color vision in one of two ways: the trichromatic theory and the opponent process theory.

Thomas Young, a nineteenth-century English scientist, suggested that it takes just three colors for us to see all the colors of the spectrum. He demonstrated this through experiments where he showed that people could match any color by making a combination of just three wavelengths, or colors, of light. It's similar to a color-wheel explanation of vision—taking just three colors and blending them together in different combinations will make any color. Surprisingly, this theory emerged 70 years before anyone knew that humans have three different kinds of retina cones—blue, green, and red (Figure 3.3).

Not all scientists, however, agreed with the trichromatic theory. By the late 1800s, some scientists thought that it took four colors—red, green, yellow, and blue—instead of three to get our complete color vision. This became known as the opponent-process theory. This theory suggests that color vision comes from opposing processes from blue and yellow and from red and green. Scientists believed that these colors work in pairs because of a simple finding: A person staring into a red light and then looking at a white surface will see a green spot on the surface, and viewing a green light creates a red spot. By contrast, looking at a blue light generates a yellow spot, and vice versa. In certain ways, though, both of these theories explain some visual phenomena. At the retina, the cones do really work

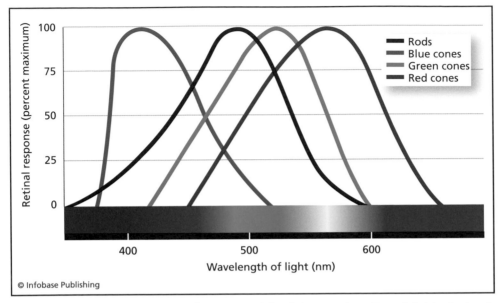

Figure 3.3 The rods in the retina respond best to wavelengths of light at about the middle of the range that humans can see. There are three different types of cones, which respond best to blue, green, or red wavelengths of light. This explains why our visual system sometimes behaves according to the trichromatic theory of color vision.

like the trichromatic theory suggests, allowing us to see all the colors in the visible spectrum. At higher levels of the visual system, opponent processing emerges.

PERCEIVING SIZE AND DEPTH

The visual system uses some general rules to decide how far away things might be (Figure 3.4). Although many people believe that depth perception requires two eyes, just one eye can give a few clues to distance, too. For example, if one object covers up another, a person observing them assumes that the covered object is farther away. Also, what a person knows about an object affects the perception of distance. If a quarter and a dime appear to be the same size, you would conclude that the

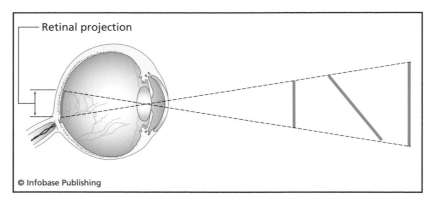

Figure 3.4 The size of the retinal image—the actual distance that a viewed object covers on the surface of the retina—can be the same for different objects. For example, a more distant quarter, a closer dime, and a tilted quarter at a middle distance can all cover the same surface area of the retina.

quarter is farther away, because you know that a quarter is larger than a dime. A person can also judge distance with just one eye by using motion parallax, which describes the fact that moving things appear to go slower if they are far away. Think of being at a car race. When a car roars down the straightaway right in front of you, it might move so fast that it makes a blur in your visual perception. But when the car reaches the back stretch, it appears to go more slowly and does not blur.

Using two eyes to see also helps a person determine distance. Binocular disparity—when an image appears slightly shifted on one retina versus the other—provides information about distance. In essence, objects that are farther away tend to land on about the same area in both retinas; closer things tend to land in more different, or disparate, places on the two retinas. The brain can use those differences to help judge distance.

One key to figuring out size and distance comes from the principle of size constancy. This means that a person perceives the same item as always being the same size. Think back to the beginning of this book, to the experiment with the quarters.

Even though the quarter farther from your eye would make a smaller image on your retina, your brain somehow magnifies the perception so that the two quarters look to be the same size. One could also judge an object's size by comparing it to the size of something that he or she already knows. For example, if

Binocular Rivalry

As mentioned in the description of binocular disparity, a person's two eyes see images at different places on the retina. To prove this, hold a finger in front of your face and close your right eye, and then open it and close your left eye. Your finger seems to move back and forth because the image lands on different spots of your two retinas. In some cases, your brain uses this information together, such as when judging distance through binocular disparity. In other cases, your brain focuses on the information from one eye over the other. This is an example of binocular rivalry.

To demonstrate binocular rivalry, get a cardboard tube from a roll of paper towels and hold it against your right eye, looking through it as though it is a telescope. Then, hold your left hand about four inches from your left eye, with your palm facing toward you and just barely touching the tube. At first, you should perceive a hole through your left hand because your brain focuses on the information from your right eye. In just a few seconds, though, that hole seems filled in, with a somewhat fuzzy continuation of your palm, as the brain focuses on the information from your left eye. Keep looking. Eventually, the two images—left hand with a hole and left hand with fuzzy, filled-in hole—switch back and forth. Your brain alternates between the two perceptions.

something unknown lies beside a quarter, one can estimate the unknown item's size in comparison to the quarter's size.

Still, humans do not always judge size correctly, as the Ponzo illusion reveals. Other illusions also show how size perception can be tricked. For example, an image called the Müller-Lyer illusion depicts two lines side by side. One has outward-pointing arrowheads on each end, and the other has inward-pointing arrowheads. Even when the lines are exactly the same length, the line with inward-pointing arrowheads looks longer (Figure 3.5). No one knows for sure why this happens, but humans probably interpret the size of the lines on how objects usually appear in nature.

UNDERSTANDING MOTION

Perceiving motion might be one of a person's most crucial skills. For any animal, seeing motion is a key to survival. Many animals, such as rabbits, first try to escape danger by not moving. But if a nearby predator makes a quick move, the rabbit usually flees. This is because the rabbit's visual system responds to the motion and the knowledge that something moving could be dangerous. Humans react to movement in a similar way. People duck, jump, or run after catching a glimpse of a fast, oncoming object.

Humans see at least two kinds of motion: real and induced. Real motion is seen while watching something that truly moves, such as someone going by on a bicycle. Induced motion is perceived when a person thinks something stationary is moving because something else around it moves. For example, if one looks at the Moon at night, it appears stationary in the sky. But if wind blows clouds across the moon, the Moon appears to move the opposite way. This is induced motion, because the racing clouds make it appear as if the Moon is moving. You

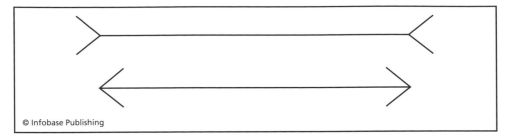

Figure 3.5 In the above illustration, the upper line looks longer than the lower one, but they are the same length. Like the Ponzo illusion, there is no consensus among scientists about why we perceive this as we do.

can also feel like you are moving even when you are not, due to the perception of induced movement. When you are sitting in your car at a stoplight and the car next to you moves, you catch it in your peripheral vision and can feel like your own car is rolling. The perception can feel so real that you might even push hard on your brakes to "stop."

One kind of movement in the visual system, though, goes completely unnoticed. This movement is called saccades and is the rapid back-and-forth movements of the eyes. Human eyes do this constantly, but if a person actually noticed it, the world would appear jittery as his eyes scanned side to side. A person doesn't notice the saccades because his brain suppresses that information. Scientists have found specific neurons in the brain that get turned off during saccades. It's as if the eyes are scanning the environment constantly, perhaps to keep track of what's going on in the world. But most of this information goes unrecognized.

It might seem that saccades go unnoticed just because they happen too fast. Experiments show, however, that the human visual system can see things at the speed of saccades. This provides more evidence that humans must suppress that information in order to ignore it.

TELLING ITEMS APART

It can be difficult to fully understand how the brain interprets an image. It involves the behavior of neurons in the primary visual cortex, plus the processes that allow humans to interpret size, distance, and motion. There are many factors that work together to assemble all the bits and pieces of neural information to, say, recognize a face. Moreover, science still needs to learn more to understand this level of visual perception.

Development of Visual Perception

Human infants can see little at birth. Even by one month of age, visual acuity reaches only 20/400 to 20/600, which means that a one-month-old must be within 20 feet of something to see what an adult can see at 400 to 600 feet. This arises, at least in part, because an infant's visual cortex is not completely developed. Consequently, a one-month-old cannot see much detail. Still, at just a couple of days old, an infant can recognize its mother's face.

As time goes by, infants develop more and more visual capabilities. By three months of age, an infant can use clues from motion to correctly perceive arrangements of objects. For example, if you were to hold a broomstick parallel to the ground and wiggle it up and down behind a tree, a three-month-old would know that the two ends are part of one object and that its middle was hidden behind the tree. A younger infant would likely think that the two ends of the broomstick were separate objects, since he would not understand that part of the stick was hidden behind the tree. By three months, an infant can also perceive facial expressions and smoothly follow movements with his eyes. At four months, an infant can categorize colors just like an adult. By one year, a child sees as well as an adult.

Nonetheless, some research does give insight into how humans distinguish one image from another. Some of this comes from **functional magnetic resonance imaging**, or fMRI. Without resorting to invasive surgical procedures, this technique shows which parts of the brain are active in reaction to various stimuli. While inside an fMRI machine, a person can be shown different images, such as a cat, human faces, and other objects. In such an experiment, different parts of the brain "turn on" when the different images appear. There can be some overlap between the groups of neurons that respond to different images, but the overall group of neurons that react to one stimuli differs enough from another group for the brain to distinguish one image from the other.

Given such a complex visual code, and considering how experience impacts the way humans interpret various images, scientists have long wondered if one person sees the world the same way that another person sees it. It is true that some objects look different to different people. For example, a tree appears different to someone who sees in color versus someone who is colorblind. Likewise, some people can see details that move too fast for other people to notice them.

Baseball players are one group of people who have a special ability to see fast-moving details. Professional ball players, for example, perceive specific characteristics about the spin of a pitch—a pitch that might travel close to 100 miles per hour (160 km/h) and spin a couple of thousand times per minute. The athletes use their knowledge of a ball's spin to predict its path. How much spin someone can see depends on his or her dynamic visual acuity, which is a measurement of the perception of moving objects. On average, experienced athletes possess better dynamic **visual acuity** than most nonathletes. Although some athletes are born with a heightened ability for this, it seems that it can also be enhanced through training.

To understand how excellent visual acuity can develop, picture this: A record player spins a record at 33 revolutions per minute. Most people can read the label on a record spinning at that rate, but not at much faster speeds. Baseball legend Ted Williams, the great hitter for the Boston Red Sox, enjoyed better dynamic visual acuity. He could read the label on a record spinning at 78 revolutions per minute, two and a half times faster than what an average person can see.[7]

Even if some people can see certain things that others cannot, do most people see the world in more or less the same way? The answer seems to be yes—sort of. Again using fMRI, one experiment showed that while a group of people watched a movie, the same areas of everyone's brain turned on at more or less the same time. This does not necessarily mean that they all perceived the movie in exactly the same way, but it does indicate that their brains processed the information in similar locations. Not surprisingly, though, this same experiment showed some variation from one person to the next. At this point, that's about as far as science can go in answering how differently people see the world.

COMBINING SENSES

When exploring the human brain, science often studies the senses separately from each other. But in reality, life is experienced through a mixture of sensations. The movie experiment, for example, consisted of stimuli that was seen and heard, which the brain, at some level, processed together.

The human body clearly divides sensory inputs at some level, using eyes to see and ears to hear, but there is also evidence that those inputs get combined to some extent. Some neurons in the brain respond to a combination of vision and touch. In one experiment, scientists recorded neurons in the brains of monkeys. These neurons responded to a touch on a specific spot on their hands, and also to the sight of an object moving near that same spot. This demonstrates that the neurons combined information about touch or vision in the same area on the hand.

Depth perception, sensing motion, and more reveal the intrigue of visual processing. They show quite convincingly that the visual system is far more than just a camera. The combination of eyes and the visual areas in the brain create a very powerful visual-processing system—one that cannot be matched by any sort of modern technology.

■ **Learn more about the contents of this chapter** Search the Internet for *Gestalt psychology*, *color vision*, and *vision development*.

4 | Hearing

Imagine watching someone on television mouth the syllable *ga* when the sound on the TV plays the syllable *ba*. Logically, it would make sense that you would hear *ba*. But in fact, people often hear the syllable *da*. This is called the McGurk effect, and it shows that perceiving speech depends on more than just hearing. Somehow, the brain combines seeing the mouthing of *ga* and hearing *ba* to perceiving *da*. No one knows exactly what causes this to happen, but it reveals that vision also impacts what people hear, at least when it comes to listening to what someone says.

Understanding hearing, though, requires some knowledge of **sound**. At a basic level, sound develops when something vibrates. The sounds that one hears come from vibrating air. Vibrations travel in waves that can be described by their **frequency**. Imagine being able to watch sounds waves and counting the number of waves that go by in one second—that is the wave's frequency, or cycles per second. Frequency is measured in units called hertz (Hz). Humans can hear sounds that range from about 20 to 20,000 Hz. As frequency increases, so does the pitch of the sound. The loudness of a sound relates to the amplitude (height) of the wave. Loudness is measured in units called decibels (dB) that relate to how hard sound waves push on the ear. A watch tick is about 20 dB, normal talking is 50 dB, and a jet engine is 130 dB.

In order to hear sound, it must first be captured. That's what the outer ear does. It guides sound waves inside, where they strike the **tympanic membrane**, or eardrum. The vibrations in the sound waves cause the tympanic membrane to vibrate. The vibration transfers the sound energy to a series of three small bones in the middle ear (Figure 4.1): the **malleus** (or hammer), **incus** (or anvil), and **stapes** (or stirrup). When the tympanic membrane vibrates, it moves the malleus, which in turn moves the incus, which then moves the stapes. Finally, the stapes pushes and pulls on a structure called the oval window.

FEELING THE FREQUENCY

On the other side of the oval window, all the pushing and pulling is converted into electric signals. This process takes place in the **cochlea**, which means "snail shell" in Greek. Vibration of the oval window sends waves through fluid contained within the cochlea. The waves shake the basilar membrane, which runs down the middle of the cochlea. Shaking the basilar membrane results in the creation of a wave along the membrane. The wave does not always appear on the same part of the membrane. The frequency of the sound determines where the wave appears. High frequencies move the portion of the membrane near the oval window and lower frequencies shake the far end. Sounds made of several frequencies—as nearly all sounds are—shake different parts of the basilar membrane. Such an arrangement makes up a **tonotopic map**, or a structure that maps out different frequencies, or tones. Auditory cells, called hair cells, are attached to the membrane. When stimulated, they create electric signals that are sent to the brain. The brain processes

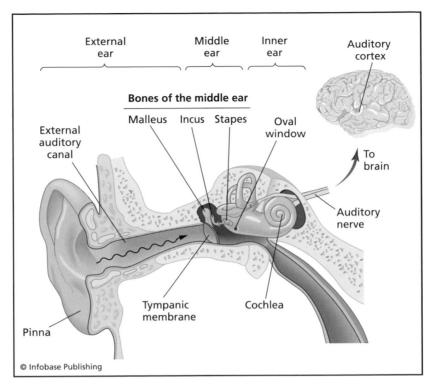

Figure 4.1 Our auditory system captures sound with the ear. Vibrations go through the eardrum and pass through three bones in the middle ear to the cochlea in the inner ear. The vibrations are then converted to electrical signals and are carried to the brain via the auditory nerve.

and interprets these signals as whatever the sound might be—music, or the sound of rushing water, or the ticking of a clock, or any of the other sounds that one might encounter.

LOCATING SOUNDS

If a person is looking straight ahead and a sound comes from his left, it reaches his left ear before it gets to the right one (Figure 4.2). The delay between when it reaches the first ear and when it reaches the second is about 600 to 700 milliseconds, or 0.6 to 0.7 seconds. The head also blocks some of the sound so it is louder on the left than the right. Humans use this sort of information to determine a sound's location.

The timing delay impacts neurons in the superior olivary nucleus (SON) in the brain stem. To understand how these neurons decode the time delay, imagine this: line up a series of neurons left to right inside the brain. Information (in the form of action potentials in neurons) from the left ear comes from the left and along the top of the line of neurons; information from the right ear comes from the right side and contacts the bottom of each neuron in the row. To get turned on, a neuron in the row needs input from the left and right ears at once. If a sound comes directly from the left, it first stimulates the left ear and its cochlea sends a signal to the row of SON cells. That information probably reaches the first SON cell before much happens on the right side. The information from the left ear moves on to the next SON cell in the line. A fraction of a second later, the sound gets around to the other side of the head (to the right ear) and the right cochlea starts sending information in from the other end of the row of SON cells. At some spot along that row, input arrives from both ears at the same time and a SON cell fires. It's like two trains racing toward each other, with one getting a head start. The one that gets started first is farther along the track before the collision. The brain can learn from experience where a sound probably comes from when certain SON cells fire.

ORGANIZING OTHER FEATURES

Parts of the auditory system often focus on particular features of sounds. The SON, for example, has time-delay neurons. It also dedicates other neurons to noting a sound's volume differences at the two ears. The time-delay neurons that help

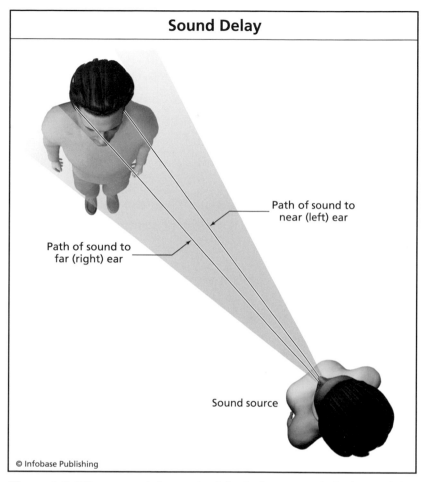

Figure 4.2 When sound does not originate from exactly in front of the listener, the vibrations reach the sound-side ear before the other ear. Our auditory system can use this information to help determine the direction of a sound's source.

determine a sound's location rely on when the sound reaches the two ears. The volume neurons respond to the pressure that reaches the two ears. The differences in volume at the two ears, though, could also be used in parts of the brain to help determine location.

Many locations in the brain are concerned with sound frequency. For example, frequency maps, like those in the basilar membrane in the cochlea, turn up again in the SON and in several parts of the auditory cortex. No one knows exactly why our brain breaks sounds into its component frequencies multiple times. Other animals, including bats, have many areas in their brains that process sound frequencies. Perhaps this gives those animals even more information about the kinds of sounds that they hear.

Some of the most interesting auditory areas are the ones that map out the space around an animal. Scientists have studied

Echolocation in Bats

Bats, the group known as Microchiroptera, have an amazing sensory capability called echolocation. It works like this: A bat makes a sound that echoes back after it strikes an object. The bat interprets its surroundings from the information received in the echoes. A bat uses these signals to avoid obstacles as it flies and hunts prey, such as insects. By scanning with ultrasound, a bat can find a flying insect's location and even get a good idea of its size based mostly on the loudness of an echo reflected off the insect. Some other animals, including dolphins, whales, and some birds, also use echolocation.

People cannot hear a bat's echolocation calls because the calls consist of frequencies beyond the range of human hearing. Humans, at least young ones, can hear sounds up to about 20,000 Hz, and bat calls can surpass 100,000 Hz. A bat's returning echo carries more information than loudness.

The frequency of the echo also affects how a bat interprets the information it receives. When a bat sends out echolocating

this very carefully in barn owls. These owls need some way to locate sounds accurately, because they usually hunt in the dark. Although they have exceptional night vision, barn owls also have an excellent sense of hearing. A barn owl perched in a completely dark lab can hear a mouse scurry across the floor and swoop down and capture it with relative ease.

The owl can do this because its brain contains maps of auditory space. That is, parts of its brain serve as three-dimensional maps of the auditory world that surrounds it. Imagine that the owl is inside a big sphere and hears a sound upward and to the right. There is a similar, but much smaller, sphere of tissue in

calls, it knows the frequency that it sent and it has elaborate tonotopic maps in its brain to determine the frequency of the returning echoes. This echo contains more information about an insect. If a call comes back with the frequency increased, the insect is flying toward the bat, but if the frequency comes back lower, then the insect is flying away. Some research suggests that bats can distinguish fluttering wings through echolocation and can tell what kind of insect it is pursuing.

Some animals listen for the echolocating calls of bats. For example, many night-flying insects, including crickets, moths, praying mantids, and even some beetles, can hear the calls of bats. When they do, they fly away. If the ultrasound is particularly loud, suggesting that the bat is close, some insects display amazing aerobatics, flying through loops, swerving violently, and spiraling to the ground in order to escape.

the owl's brain, and a neuron fires in the area of the brain that corresponds with where the sound was located. The neuron shows the angle (left or right), the elevation (up or down), and the distance to the sound. That is how the barn owl knows the exact location of the mouse.

SPEECH PERCEPTION

Phonemes make up the shortest segments of speech that can be changed to make us perceive one word versus another. Phonemes are not letters; they're sounds, such as the vowel sound in *sweet* and *heat.* English uses 13 vowel-sound phonemes. For a vowel-sound phoneme, consider the difference in the sounds for the words *heed* and *hid.* Then, there are 24 consonant-sound phonemes in English, such as the *p* sound in *pull* or the *b* sound in *bull.*

Depending on the language, the number of phonemes varies, and it can even vary between speakers. This creates a difficulty in understanding speech. If one were to build a system to understand speech, one might consider recording all of the words in a language and then writing a computer program that looks for the frequency of the words and so on. That is, it would make sense to build a system that could identify the "acoustic signature" of each word. The problem is, that acoustical signature—even for the same word—will vary between people. That's why voice-recognition software—a computer program that allows a person to speak commands instead of entering them on a keyboard—works better after it can be trained to work for one particular user. The software tries to learn how that one person talks. These kinds of programs would work easier if all people talked the same, but even the *same* person does not always say a word the same way.

Because of these types of complexities, the brain looks for ways to simplify and better understand sensory stimuli.

Categorical perception provides one approach. This capability of the brain draws imaginary lines between different sounds; that is, it helps the brain divide sounds into categories. A common example of this phenomenon involves the sounds *ba* and *pa*. One distinction between these two sounds is called voice-onset time, or the time from the start of saying a sound until your vocal cords start vibrating. That's correct: the sound can start first, and then the cords get into the act. For the sound *ba*, the cords vibrate right away, but there is a bit of a delay for the sound *pa*. So the voice-onset delay is shorter for *ba*, longer for *pa*. If scientists vary the voice-onset delay, we do not perceive endless variations of sounds. Instead, for the shorter voice-onset delays, we perceive *ba*, and for longer ones, we perceive *pa*. To clean up the entire mess of possible sounds, the human brain just makes two categories. Then when it hears a variation on either of these sounds, it does not need to choose between millions of possibilities. It's a *ba* or it's a *pa*—that's all there is to it.

Categorical perception is part of the reason why someone from Alabama can understand someone from New York City, even though those two people have very different accents. In some cases, even categorical perception is not enough. Much of speech recognition relies on experience. The more a person hears a certain sound, the easier it is to understand. To prove this point, just ask your parents to decipher one line of music from your favorite song. It's easy enough for you to understand, but it could sound like a Martian language to them.

Recent research also shows that the brain can encode the exact same sound in different ways. The brain can hear the word *yes* twice and, it seems, turn on distinctly different neurons when it hears the word on different occasions. This further puzzles scientists as the work to figure out how the brain tells the difference between two similar-sounding words.

Understanding words, though, might not always be about hearing. One group of scientists showed that literally feeling the beat of music impacted the hearing of music in infants. How the infants moved while listening to music with a strong beat actually affected the auditory encoding of that beat. These scientists concluded that body movement impacts the perception of rhythm in music.

■ **Learn more about the contents of this chapter** Search the Internet for *auditory perception*, *echolocation*, and *speech perception*.

5 | Smell

A whiff of a certain perfume can remind someone, even decades later, of a person he or she once knew. The rustic smell of a pile of leaves can bring back childhood memories so intense that they seem to have happened just hours ago, although the memory is many, many years old. The ability to harbor smell memories for so many years has puzzled scientists, because key neurons in the olfactory (smell) system live for only about 60 days. Clearly, something in this system lasts much longer.

Understanding the source of smell memories requires knowledge of the entire olfactory system (Figure 5.1). Moreover, smell fits into a different category than vision and hearing, which sense photons and sound waves, respectively. Olfaction—the sense of smell—is a chemical sense because odors consist of chemicals. Photons or sound waves cannot be smelled. Humans use the sense of smell for many reasons, such as avoiding dangerous things (smoke in a burning building), locating food (like the smell of pancakes cooking on a Saturday morning), and recognizing familiar places.

These capabilities start with the nose, which collects molecules from the air. Once inside, the molecules dissolve on the **olfactory epithelium**, which is located inside the nose, behind the bridge. Receptors on hair cells respond to specific

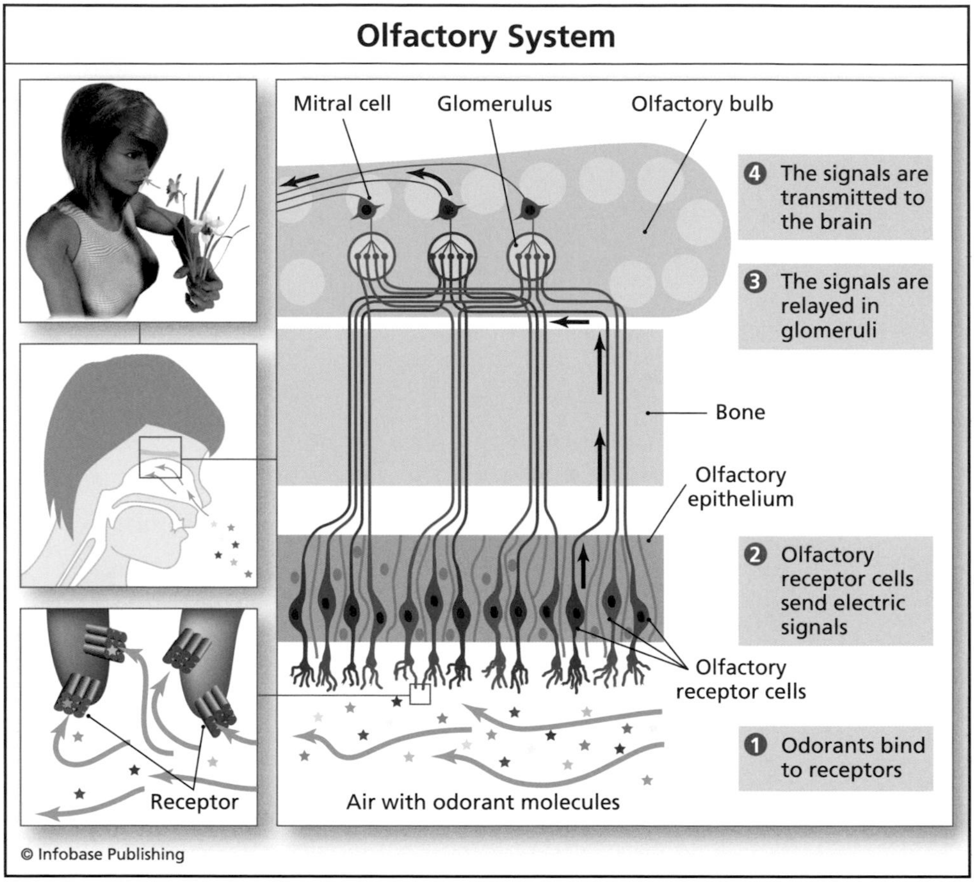

Olfactory System

Mitral cell   Glomerulus   Olfactory bulb

❹ The signals are transmitted to the brain

❸ The signals are relayed in glomeruli

Bone

Olfactory epithelium

❷ Olfactory receptor cells send electric signals

Olfactory receptor cells

❶ Odorants bind to receptors

Receptor   Air with odorant molecules

© Infobase Publishing

Figure 5.1 Odor molecules come in through the nose, where they can be picked up by the olfactory epithelium. The olfactory receptor cells send signals to the olfactory bulb in the brain for further processing, and then the information goes to higher-brain areas.

chemicals that are absorbed by the olfactory epithelium. The human nose has about 40 million receptor cells. In dogs, whose noses are more sensitive to smells than those of humans, there are a couple of billion receptor cells.[8] It is not entirely clear how a chemical interacts with olfactory receptors. Maybe the receptors work like locks, and the molecules serve as keys that open—or "turn on"—specific receptors. Information from the chemicals in the air triggers activity in olfactory receptors that pass the information to the **olfactory bulb**, lying just above the receptors. The olfactory bulb then passes the information to a variety of locations in the brain.

OLFACTORY RECEPTORS

Humans can tell apart thousands of odors. Someone trained to distinguish scents, such as a professional perfume maker, may be able to smell as many as 10,000 different scents. Just what exactly a person can smell also depends on inherited factors. Some people even suffer from anosmia, the lack of ability to smell.

In 1991, two scientists—Linda B. Buck of the Fred Hutchinson Cancer Research Center and Richard Axel of Columbia University Medical School—published a paper estimating that rats have about 1,000 genes for olfactory receptors. Humans appear to have about 350 olfactory genes, which suggests that there could be 350 different kinds of receptors. Keep in mind, though, that a single receptor can respond to more than one odor molecule. Likewise, a single odor probably activates more than one receptor. Buck and Axel also showed that a single gene makes an individual olfactory-receptor cell. This work earned Buck and Axel the 2004 Noble Prize in Physiology or Medicine.

EXPLORING THE OLFACTORY BULB

About 10 million neurons connect the olfactory epithelium[9] to the olfactory bulb, which in humans is the size of a pea. The olfactory bulb consists of layers of neurons that process odor information (Figure 5.2). The outermost layers of the bulb include sphere-shaped structures called glomeruli, each of which receives input from a specific type of receptor cell. Since any odor will activate more than one kind of receptor cell in the olfactory epithelium, that same odor turns on a combination of

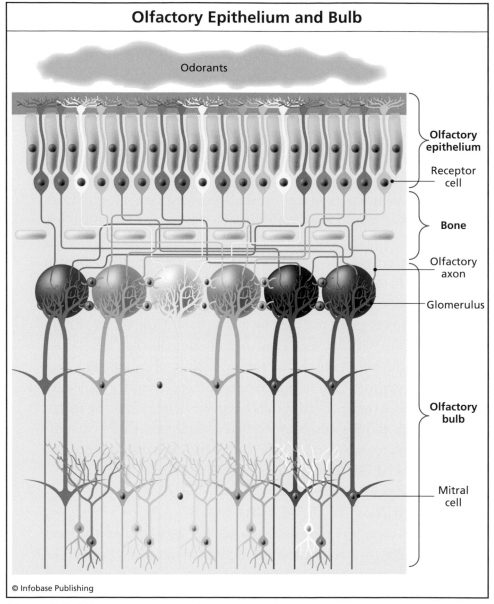

Olfactory Epithelium and Bulb

Odorants

Olfactory epithelium

Receptor cell

Bone

Olfactory axon

Glomerulus

Olfactory bulb

Mitral cell

© Infobase Publishing

Figure 5.2 Olfactory receptors that express the same gene connect to the same glomerulus in the olfactory bulb. One of a kind receptor—for example, the ones coded red in the illustration—go to the same glomerulus, also shown in red. Consequently, the glomeruli make an odor map, which gets passed to mitral cells that take the information to the brain.

glomeruli in the olfactory bulb. Different odors turn on different combinations of glomeruli, and that pattern of excitation represents a particular smell. The identification—perceiving a smell and knowing what it is—takes place in other parts of the brain.

The identification of smell can play a role in communication. Mice, for example, can smell a chemical in urine that helps them tell male mice from female mice. This chemical only exists in a male mouse's urine, and smelling it activates neurons in a mouse's olfactory bulb. Although the mouse urine contains hundreds of compounds, just one neuron in their olfactory bulbs signals the presence or absence of the male urine signature. That one neuron serves as a "feature detector" of sorts. A mouse's brain could look at the response of that neuron and ask: Is it on or off? If the neuron is on, the mouse's brain would know that a male mouse is nearby; if it is off, there is no male around.

The communication is indicated by the fact that female mice show a real interest when they smell the male urine compound. But it's not just that male component that makes the females active. They must get the male smell along with a general urine odor. So the general smell of urine plus the male-specific component creates a complete communication turn on for the females.

IDENTIFYING MIXTURES

Most olfactory experiences involve more than one odor at once. For the most part, the human olfactory system faces a buffet of odors. Also, combinations of odors can even make a person perceive new ones.

Here's an example of a new combination. When people smell a chemical called eugenol, it smells like cloves. Another compound, phenylethyl alcohol, smells like roses. When sniffing eugenol along with phenylethyl alcohol, some people say it smells like carnations. In other words, our olfactory system takes two separate smells and makes a third one that is completely different.

Some research into the mouse olfactory system suggests how this odor morphing might occur. By watching the activity of cells in a mouse's olfactory cortex, scientists can see which ones are activated by different odors. If one odor turns on one population of cells in the olfactory cortex and another odor turns on a different population of cells, then, as some experiments show, stimulating the mouse with both odors at once will activate a third population of cells. This could be the mechanism that turns the smells of roses and cloves together into that of carnations. It might sound like olfactory magic, but it's really just how the nervous system categorizes different combinations of smells.

The results described so far suggest that the initial stages of the olfactory system—especially the olfactory epithelium—sort out the compounds in odors. As the information gets passed along, moving into the brain, the information seems to be recombined. Several areas of the brain receive information about smells. The information goes to the primary olfactory cortex, which is basically on the underside of the brain, about three-quarters of the way to the back. The secondary olfactory cortex, located in the frontal lobe, also processes smell information. Smell information also goes to the amygdala, which is inside the temporal lobe. This structure seems to be related to the memory of smells. Eventually, the brain puts all the information together to decide on the cause of the smell.

MORE THAN SMELL

Odors impact more than just olfaction. To prove that, try this experiment: Get a bowl of jellybeans, close your eyes, pinch your nose, and take an unidentified flavor of bean from the bowl and eat it. What flavor did you pick? With your nose pinched, none of the jellybean-odor molecules can reach your olfactory epithelium, and you probably can't recognize the bean's flavor. You might taste the sweetness, but nothing else.

The World's Best Smellers

Virtually all animals can smell, or at least sense chemicals in some way. Sometimes the best smellers surprise us. Among sensory biologists, sharks get respect not just for their potential bite, but for their sense of smell, too. When a shark swims, water moves through two nostrils, and then flows along folds of skin that contain receptors. Many sharks develop a particularly good sense of smell for blood. Some research indicates that sharks can smell one drop of blood in an area of water the size of a swimming pool.

Other marine animals also possess significant olfactory capabilities. Some skates can smell tiny amounts of particular chemicals, including some amino acids, the building blocks for proteins. In fact, a skate's sense of smell can be so good, some sources suggest that this animal could smell out two tablespoons of a chemical in the Scottish lake Loch Ness, which covers about 21 square miles (54 square kilometers) and is an average of about 430 feet (131 m) deep.

When most people think of the best smellers, though, dogs usually come to mind. When police officers bring dogs to track a fugitive in a swamp or find bombs at an airport, it's obvious that these animals can really use their noses. According to James Walker, director of the Sensory Research Institute at Florida State University in Tallahassee, a dog's sense of smell is about 10,000 to 100,000 times better than that of humans.[10] Walker adds that a dog's brain applies much more of its resources to smell than does a human's brain.

In real life, you rarely just taste something. You smell at the same time. To complete the experiment, keep your eyes closed but let your nose in on the action this time. Take another unknown jellybean and try to identify the flavor. It should be much easier now. You detect the sweetness with your tongue, and your olfactory system tries to identify the odor.

The seemingly unrelated systems for sensation and perception reveal some common patterns of processing. For example, many of the sensory systems start to interpret information by breaking it into components. Cones divide light into different frequencies, the cochlea spreads sounds into different frequencies, and the olfactory epithelium splits odors into different compounds. At higher levels, though, sensory systems put information back together to identify things around us. It's like fixing something mechanical: you often need to take it apart before putting it back together. A similar process might help the human sensory systems know as much about a sensation as possible.

■ **Learn more about the contents of this chapter** Search the Internet for *olfactory memory*, *olfactory receptor*, and *olfactory cortex*.

6 | Taste

There's more on the tip of your tongue than you might imagine. Scientists at Yale University stimulated peoples' tongues with temperature, and they experienced tastes. Part of this finding is old news. Years ago, scientists discovered that the nerves from the tongue that respond to taste are also activated by temperature. No one knew how the brain interprets different temperatures on the tongue. The Yale scientists dubbed this "thermal taste." In general, scientists categorize taste into four different forms: salty, sweet, sour, and bitter. A more recently recognized taste called umami (pronounced oo-ma-mi) also exists. We perceive umami when we eat certain salts, such as mono-sodium glutamate (MSG), which is used in many packaged foods, such as dried soup.

The Yale scientists found that temperature changes on the tongue could make people perceive some basic forms of taste: salty, sweet, bitter, and sour. Depending on where the temperature change is applied to the tongue, the taste perception varies. In general, heating up the tongue's tip tastes sweet, the side triggers a sour taste, and the back stimulates a bitter perception. Only some people experience thermal taste, and sweetness is the most common sensation. For some people, just touching the tongue to an ice cube can generate a salty perception. In most cases, though, the tongue responds to food more than temperature.

Taste is more than just identifying food flavors. Taste can help trigger an appetite, for example. Just imagining the taste of a certain food can make a person crave it. But taste also protects us. For example, people tend to avoid bitter things, and most poisons generate a bitter perception. Likewise, most people do not like anything too sour, and food turns sour when it spoils. As is the case with other forms of sensation and perception that develop with experience, people also learn what foods to eat and which ones to avoid. Similarly, some of the hardwiring in the taste system teaches people to like and dislike most of the right things from the start. Some tastes might drive a person to eat what is needed at a particular time. If your body feels tired, someone might crave sweets; carbo-hydrates taste sweet, and the body needs carbohydrates to run. Also, salt keeps a person from dehydrating, and people might crave salt when feeling thirsty. Umami might drive the body's need for protein.

A TOUR OF THE TONGUE

Stick out your tongue and look at it closely in a mirror. It is cov-ered with tiny bumps that make it look a bit like velvet. Some of these bumps contain collections of cells called **taste buds.** They exist all over most of the tongue and throughout the mouth area. On the tongue, though, the most common bumps are for touch, not taste.

One bud consists of many taste cells, usually 40 to 100 of them.[11] Each taste cell reaches through the taste bud with little projections. These taste cell "fingers" poke out through a pore in the taste bud. There the taste cells—or receptors—can interact with the food in a person's mouth.

Within one taste bud, there are cells for every kind of taste perception, and just a single taste receptor can respond to more than one taste. Consequently, the machinery for tasting different things is spread all over the tongue. The nerves that carry taste information to the brain also connect with more than one taste cell. In the end, though, the perception of taste lies in the brain.

REVVING UP THE RECEPTORS

Table salt consists of two elements: sodium and chloride. In water, the salt breaks into the two components. When something salty hits the tongue, the sodium can enter a salt receptor to start the process that activates the cell (Figure 6.1).

Sour foods release protons, a part of an atom that carries a positive electrical charge. Protons can block some of the pores in a sour receptor, which can cause the neuron to fire, signaling a sour perception. Sweet receptors work differently. Sugar attaches to a molecule on the surface of the taste receptor. This sets off a chain reaction of processes inside the cell that eventually causes the cell to turn on. Bitter substances work like sweet ones, by attaching to a molecule on the receptor's surface and setting off a series of reactions inside the cell. Not surprisingly, the exact reactions inside taste receptors differ for the sweet and bitter sensations. With umami (the taste we perceive when eating something containing MSG) it's not the salt that triggers the sensation. Instead, amino acids from the umami-generating food attach to molecules on the receptor's surface. As with sweet and bitter foods, the binding sets off activity inside the receptor that makes it respond.

A food's class—for example, carbohydrates—does not necessarily determine its taste. Many people think of carbohydrates as being sweet foods, but not all carbohydrates are sweet. The same class of foods can trigger different taste perceptions. Likewise,

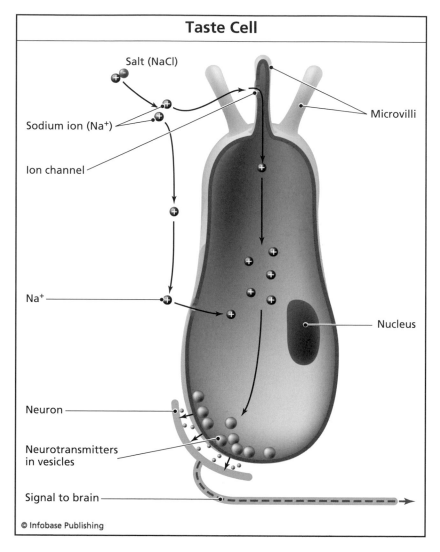

Taste Cell

Salt (NaCl)

Sodium ion (Na⁺)

Ion channel

Na⁺

Neuron

Neurotransmitters
in vesicles

Signal to brain

Microvilli

Nucleus

© Infobase Publishing

Figure 6.1 When a person puts something salty in his or her mouth, sodium ions from the salt enter taste cells. This action causes the release of neurotransmitters, which turns on neurons that take the information to the brain.

different classes can create the same perceptions. For example, the artificial sweetener aspartame is not at all like a sugar, but it tastes sweet.

THE GENETICS OF TASTE

The same food can often taste very different to different people. In fact, there are some substances that only certain people can taste. An example of this situation was discovered in a laboratory at the DuPont Company in 1931. When a chemist mixed a particular combination of substances, part of it blew into the air. A nearby colleague immediately noted the bitterness of the chemical, but the chemist tasted nothing. That chemical was phenylthiocarbamide, better known simply as PTC—a compound that is artificial, and typically only encountered today in taste tests.

The ability or inability to taste PTC is genetic; in other words, it runs in families. If your parents can taste PTC, you probably can, too. If your parents can't taste PTC, you probably can't, either. The hereditary link between PTC tasters and nontasters was used as a paternity test before the invention of DNA fingerprinting. Of course, PTC tasting is not nearly as conclusive as DNA testing when it comes to determining a child's parents. Nonetheless, scientists did eventually find the hereditary link behind PTC. A single gene determines who can and cannot taste PTC. This gene comes in three forms. Different combinations of the forms of this gene create different kinds of taste receptors. One genetic combination makes PTC taste very bitter, while another combination leads to a slightly bitter perception, and the third triggers no perception at all.

A person's genetics also impact other aspects of taste. For example, a person's genetics affect how alcohol tastes. Some people perceive alcohol as more sweet and less bitter than do other people. Some research suggests that genetic variation might explain these differences.

TASTE IN THE BRAIN

All the parts of the taste system respond to more than one stimulus. As was already mentioned, taste buds can respond to more than one stimulus, such as salty and sweet. Also, the neurons that carry information away from the taste buds respond to more than one kind of stimulus. Not surprisingly, taste cells in the brain also are activated by multiple types of taste sensations. In most cases, though, all these neurons respond more to one kind of taste than to others.

Experiments performed in the 1940s by Carl Pfaffmann of Brown University showed that sensory neurons coming from the tongue respond to more than one taste. The information from the tongue goes first to the brain stem and is then distributed to many parts of the brain, including to the cerebral cortex. It seems that different parts of the brain work—

Exposing the Taste Map

If you read about taste in old books or even on many current Web sites, you might find a diagram of the tongue with the basic tastes outlined in different spots. These diagrams will show sweet at the tip, salty along the edges of the tip, sour along the sides about midway back, and bitter all the way at the back (Figure 6.2). Don't waste any time memorizing the picture. It's wrong.

It is odd that this idea of a tongue map is so old and has been considered wrong for decades, and yet it still hangs around. The maps even started out wrong. They came from research done in the late 1800s, which was interpreted incorrectly and ended up being drawn as a taste map a couple of decades later. As the information in this chapter shows, all types of basic taste come from all over the tongue, and the inside of the oral cavity in general. So there is no map of taste that can be broken down on the tongue. The different types of receptor cells are as mixed up as the food one chews. It only gets put back together—into a complete perception—when the brain combines all the information.

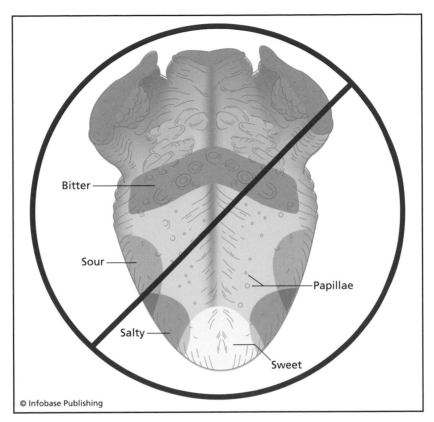

Figure 6.2 Many sources show basic tastes located in specific areas of the tongue, but this is not correct. All tastes can be picked up all over the tongue. Sometimes—like with this supposed taste map—wrong information gets perpetuated for years.

perhaps together—to help a person recognize what he or she eats. Pfaffmann's experiments suggested that the taste system might distinguish flavors through a pattern of activity, instead of just a single "light" that goes on in the brain to recognize, say, a hamburger. By the 1970s and 1980s, though, scientists started to learn that taste neurons do play favorites. That is, they react more strongly to particular stimuli. From this, scientists wondered if the taste system might recognize foods through what are called labeled lines. In other words, information about sweetness might get collected in a series of neurons—called "lines" in this hypothesis—that respond mostly to sweet tastes. There would be other lines for other tastes.

In looking at the activity of taste neurons, it appears that foods that taste the same trigger similar patterns of activity. So even if there are labeled lines, some part of the brain must interpret the activity in many of them—the pattern—to recognize a food. Instead of a labeled-line interpretation, some scientists call this the across-neurons hypothesis. The perception of taste could arise from some combination of labeled lines and across-neuron mechanisms.

Although questions remain about precisely how the brain recognizes tastes, evidence shows that the nervous system definitely keeps track of how things taste. This becomes quite clear when looking at how fast a person can learn to react to tastes. If someone eats something that makes her sick, she quickly learns to avoid it. In some experiments, scientists found that tasting something bad just once is enough to make a person avoid that food in the future. Unfortunately, this does not always work, especially when a chemical or emotional addiction comes into play. Alcoholics, for example, can get sick from drinking over and over, but they continue drinking alcohol.

FLAVOR: THE INTERACTION OF SMELL AND TASTE

The jellybean experiment in the previous chapter showed how smells impact tastes. In fact, some scientists believe that most of a person's sense of taste comes from smell. The combination of smells and tastes leads to flavor—the overall perception. Most people have experienced the impact of smell on flavor. A head cold can quickly make everything taste bland. That's because a stuffy nose prevents a food's odor molecules from activating cells in the olfactory epithelium.

Anything that goes into a person's mouth can also reach the olfactory epithelium, or at least molecules in the air can. Think about it: When someone gets a whiff of a good dinner, he might say, "That sure smells good." When he finally gets a bite, that same mingling of smells impacts how the food really does taste. The smell does not affect what the taste buds sense, but it contributes to the complete experience in his brain. Many prepared foods, such as artificially flavored candy, get different flavors from added scents alone.

If you were having trouble imagining how five kinds of taste on the tongue could create such a rich world of flavor—from your mom's homemade cookies to peanuts at a baseball game to chocolate cake at a birthday party—now you know the answer. It's your nose. The virtually limitless combinations of odors that food can produce combine with the basic tastes to create flavor.

If humans' final perception of flavor combines information from two different senses, it's clear to see why the brain must process a collection of information to figure out what a person is eating. That probably explains, too, why so many areas of the brain participate in taste. A person needs to make many decisions about what goes in his or her mouth. Is it dangerous? Is it tasty? Is it something that might cause sickness? This is why taste plays such a crucial role in survival.

■ **Learn more about the contents of this chapter** Search the Internet for *genetics of taste*, *taste receptors*, and *flavor and taste*.

7 | Touch

In the 1960s, Geerat J. Vermeij attended Princeton University. After he earned his undergraduate degree, he wanted to continue his studies in graduate school and research mollusks, such as clams, mussels, and oysters. Unfortunately, many graduate schools rejected Vermeij. They all rejected him for the same reason: He is blind.

Finally, Edgar Boell, then director of the biology graduate school program at Yale University, granted Vermeij an interview. Soon after Vermeij arrived, Boell took the prospective student to the university museum. Boell took out a shell there, handed it to Vermeij, and asked him to identify it. Vermeij felt it carefully, noted its features through touch alone, and identified the shell. Boell quickly gave Vermeij another. He identified that one, too—just by feeling the shape, size, and grooves on the shell. Vermeij was admitted to the graduate program and earned his Ph.D. in 1971.

Despite his blindness, or perhaps because of it, Vermeij built a productive career. He became a distinguished professor at the University of California at Davis, where he studies the ecology and evolutionary history of marine organisms. In his career, he has published more than 160 scientific articles and 5 books. He received the Daniel Giraud Elliot Medal from the National Academy of Sciences and was honored with a MacArthur Award—often called the "genius award." If you ever wonder just what someone can do without sight, remember Vermeij's story. Touch can be a powerful tool.

A SUMMARY OF THE SKIN

A person uses touch to determine what he contacts or what contacts him. Using his hands, a person can determine an object's size, shape, and texture. This capability comes from the skin; or, more specifically, specialized receptors in the skin pick up various forms of mechanical stimuli—how the skin gets pressed or stretched. Some of these receptors wrap around a hair's base, and they detect even very slight movements. In addition, everyone's sense of touch varies from one spot on the body to another.

The skin consists of two layers: the **epidermis** and the **dermis**. The epidermis lies on the outside in contact with the environment. Several kinds of cells make up this tissue, but it does not receive any blood vessels. The epidermis itself can also be divided into several layers. The deepest layer generates new cells, which move farther outward and turn into different kinds of epidermal cells along the way as they mature. Eventually, these cells reach the outside layer and, finally, get rubbed off.

In contrast to the epidermis, the dermis does contain blood vessels. It also includes hair cells, muscles, and nerves. A person gets goose bumps when muscles in the dermis contract, pulling hair cells up like raising flags all over the skin. Sweat glands also lie in the dermis. The hypodermis—not usually considered part of the skin—lies beneath the dermis and holds it all in place. This layer also includes fat for padding and insulation.

GETTING A FEEL FOR TOUCH

The real key to touch lies in the receptors scattered throughout the skin. These **mechanoreceptors** come in many forms (Figure 7.1). **Merkel receptors** are found between the epidermis and dermis as disk-shaped cells. A **Meissner corpuscle** looks like a stack of flattened disks, and they are located in the upper layer of the dermis. **Ruffini cylinders** include branched fibers, all kept inside a cylindrical structure, which lies at about the mid-depth of the dermis. Finally, **Pacinian corpuscles** look a little like tiny onions and can be found very deep in the skin. The skin also contains free nerve endings that respond to touch, and hair follicle endings that respond to movements on hair.

In addition to having different shapes and locations in the skin, these receptors also perform different functions. A key difference is how the receptors respond to a stimulus over time. Most important is how they react when stimulation is constant. A key to sensation is adaptation, or how cells respond to an ongoing stimulus and change how they fire. Some mechanoreceptors adapt slowly. For example, Merkel receptors and Ruffini cylinders tend to fire action potentials as long as the stimulus continues. Meissner receptors and Pacinian corpuscles, on the other hand, adapt quickly. They tend to react only to change. If something applies pressure that impacts one of these receptors, it turns on. As the pressure continues, these cells quickly turn off. Once the pressure stops, these receptors fire again, essentially reacting to the release of the pressure.

Because the receptors have different structures, are located in different places, and adapt differently, they also recognize different features of what a person touches. For example, Merkel receptors respond to the grooves in things that touch the skin. Pacinian corpuscles, however, do not show much response to such details. Instead, they seem to ask whether something is touching the skin and when it stops.

Overall, one can think of the classes of mechanoreceptors as responding to four kinds of stimuli. Merkel receptors react to pressure. Meissner corpuscles pick up flutters, sort of like ripples across the skin. Ruffini cylinders react to stretching the

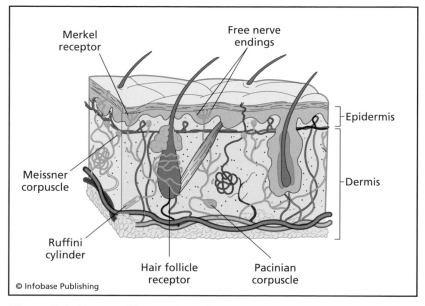

Figure 7.1 Human skin consists of two main layers: the outer epidermis and the inner dermis. This illustration also shows the different kinds of receptors that sense mechanical stimuli: Merkel receptors, Meissner corpuscles, Ruffini cylinders, Pacinian corpuscles, hair follicle receptors, and free nerve endings, which can also detect temperature.

skin. Pacinian corpuscles are activated by vibrations. Free nerve endings can respond to various kinds of touch. This gives the skin a broad arsenal of receptors to interpret a wide range of mechanical impacts.

TEMPERATURE RECEPTION

Human skin senses more than just touch. For example, it also notices temperatures, hot, cold, or in between. Some **thermoreceptors** also lie in the skin, while others are located deeper in the body. At the surface, though, temperature reception comes from the skin.

These receptors pay attention to nearby temperatures, and they come in various types, such as cold receptors and warm receptors. Cold receptors fire more rapidly as temperature goes down. They fire the most at temperatures around 77°F (25°C). Warm receptors on the other hand, fire as the temperature rises. They start firing at around 86°F (30°C). Both of these receptors adapt quickly, so they react most to temperature changes. Overall, there are more temperature receptors on a person's face and ears than anywhere else. Regardless of where a scientist looks on the body, there are more cold receptors than warm ones. In addition, so-called temperature-sensitive nociceptors respond to intense heat or cold.

Scientists still do not know exactly what areas of the brain process temperature sensations from the skin. A variety of studies indicate that information from these receptors goes to the brain's thalamus and hypothalamus. In addition, the insular cortex—which lies deep inside a fold that exists on both sides of the brain—plays some role in processing the information from temperature receptors in the skin. Other areas could be involved as well.

TOUCH PERCEPTION

Much of the processing of touch takes place in the **somatosensory cortex** (Figure 7.2). Imagine putting on headphones right across the middle of the top of your head and then pulling the band forward just a bit. The somatosensory cortex lies roughly behind where the headphones come down the side of your head but stops before reaching the level of your ear. This part of the cerebral cortex puts all the somatosensory information—from all over the body—in order. It includes a map of the sensory receptors from the entire surface of the body, but it does not look like a map drawn to scale. It is more like someone redrawing a world map, making some countries too big and others too small. Scientists call this representation a **homunculus**, and it is a distorted image of a body (Figure 7.3).

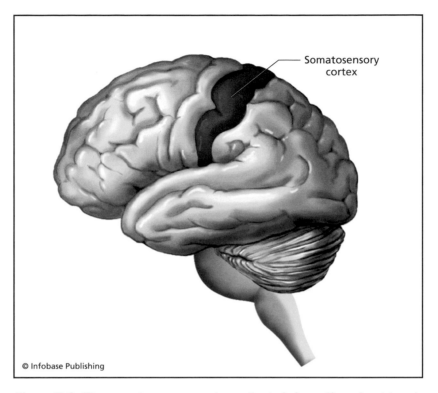

Somatosensory
cortex

© Infobase Publishing

Figure 7.2 The somatosensory cortex collects information about touch from all parts of the body.

This sensory map gets distorted because more of the cerebral cortex gets allocated to some parts of the body than it does to others. Overall, the surfaces of the body that need the most attention to the details of touch get the most space. So if you mapped out the area of the somatosensory cortex devoted to the parts of the body and then drew a person with the parts to this cortex to scale, you would get one weird-looking person. It would have a cartoonlike face; huge, puffy lips; and giant fingers. Some areas, such as the arms, trunk, and legs, would look smaller than normal.

The homunculus represents magnification in the cerebral cortex where the representations of key areas are enlarged. This

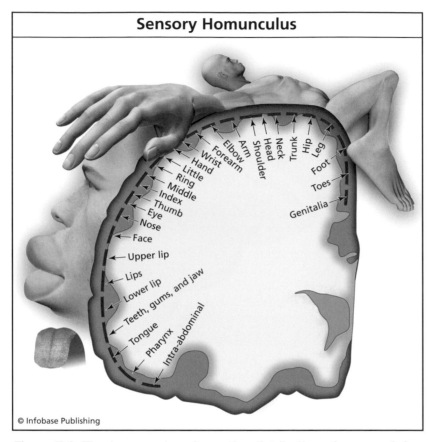

Sensory Homunculus

© Infobase Publishing

Figure 7.3 The homunculus shows the distribution of sensory information from different parts of the body. This reveals a somatosensory map of the body parts and shows which ones are more sensitive to mechanical stimuli (such as the lips, hands, and feet).

also exists in other sensory systems in the periphery and the brain. In the eye, for example, the fovea contains more cones and lets a person see more detail when he focuses an image on that part of the retina. Similarly, bats that use echolocation often use more of their auditory cortex for frequencies that matter most to them, such as those around the frequencies of their calls.

In the touch system, this magnification is related to the receptors in the skin. Areas that can touch with higher acuity—more carefully—can do that because the mechanoreceptors in those areas cover less ground. In other words, the receptive areas are smaller where we can sense smaller details. The Testing Touch Acuity sidebar shows this on pages 74–75.

FEELING OBJECTS

Even with knowledge about mechanoreceptors—knowing that some recognize pressure and others detect vibrations—and a better understanding of the receptive fields of these receptors, there is still much to explain about touch perception. How does one distinguish an apple from a baseball? How could Vermeij use only touch to tell one shell from another?

The key to understanding these questions comes from knowing that humans do not simply feel things. Instead, we explore them. Even blindfolded, a person can recognize many objects. He feels them, thinks about them, and passes them back and forth between his hands. Scientists call this **haptic perception**, which is exploring a three-dimensional object with one's hands. This ability is possible thanks to the brain's ability to combine systems. Haptic perception depends on the sensory system and the motor system, which controls movements, such as gripping a baseball. When people try to identify something through touch alone, they also think about what it might be. This system works fast—usually in a few seconds.

PAIN

Perhaps the most protective sense of all comes from pain receptors, called **nociceptors**. In the skin, these receptors exist as free nerve endings. The pain process, however, involves many aspects of the nervous system beyond the receptors. If something damages a tissue—or if the stimulus is even potentially damaging—

pain receptors turn on, and can stay on for hours, sometimes much longer. In addition, damaged tissues release a variety of chemicals that can make the pain feel even more intense.

The neurons that carry pain information enter the spinal cord where they connect to other neurons that go to the brain, to the thalamus, and then to the cerebral cortex. The cortex processes the information and determines the actual intensity of the perception of pain. Moreover, that intensity may not simply represent the magnitude of the injury. Instead, several

Testing Touch Acuity

The two-point threshold is how close two touches can be and still be perceived as two separate touches. If someone touches a pencil tip to your arm and another to your foot, you easily recognize that two pencils are touching you at once. But if someone took those two pencils and touched them close together on your back, could you tell that they were two pencils instead of one? Probably not. To test this hypothesis, pair up with a friend and get a compass, a ruler, and a piece of paper.

Pick half a dozen spots on the body—for example, the tip of your index finger, the back of your hand, your lips, your upper arm, your back, and your lower leg. Write the locations down on a piece of paper. Set the tips of the compass to be 1 millimeter apart. Have your partner touch the compass tips to the six spots and record if you feel one or two touches. Be very careful, because the tips of a compass can be very sharp. Then, set the tips to 2 millimeters, and try all of the spots again. Keep spreading the tips farther apart until you can feel two touches at every spot.

Compare the two-point thresholds to the homunculus (Figure 7.3). Areas with the smallest two-point thresholds should factors—the level of the pain stimulus, the situation, emotional factors—determine how bad the pain really feels. In a very exciting situation such as during a game, an athlete might not feel much pain from an injury. Only after the game will the athlete be aware of the pain. In one of his final tennis matches, for example, Andre Agassi fought off his back pain during the match—at least enough to stand, serve, and swing—but after the match the pain felt so intense that he had to lie down in the parking lot on his way to his car. The inhibition of pain can be

correspond to larger representations on the somatosensory cortex. So areas with more mechanoreceptors get more cortical space.

How could you improve this experiment? Perhaps you might blindfold the subjects so that they can't see the compass or where it touches them. One real key to good experimentation is making it hard for your subject to guess the right answer. So, change the order of stimuli. Write out the steps for your research, including how you will vary the order of where the assistant touches the subject's body and the distance between the compass tips. Don't just set the tips at 1 millimeter and try all the spots. Get several compasses and set them for different spacings. Then, try different spacings as you move from one spot to another. Another crucial ingredient of good research is repetition. Instead of just trying a specific compass separation once at each point, try it several times.

Remember, the best way to ask a research question—that is, how you test a hypothesis—does not always come to you immediately. You think, you experiment, you think some more, and you do more research.

an active process triggered by the brain, because it can send out signals that suppress incoming pain messages.

To show how much power the brain can exert over pain, one group of scientists put subjects under hypnosis and then observed the brain with fMRI. During this experiment, the hypnotized subjects experienced less pain than they did before being hypnotized. Also, the brain activity during pain changed for someone in that state. Even if hypnosis is not the controlling tool that it is

The Basics of a Brain Freeze

On a hot summer day, a boy gobbles down a cold bowl of ice cream. After a few bites, pain surges behind his eyes. It comes on like a bolt of lightning—so intense that it feels as if something exploded inside his head—but the bolt keeps going and going. Many people call this an ice-cream headache or a brain freeze. But before you accuse the world's ice-cream makers of causing more pain than pleasure, know that a brain freeze is not unique to eating ice cream. It can come from eating or drinking anything cold.

Usually, a brain freeze comes on quickly, just a few seconds after gulping down the cold food or drink. It builds to a peak in less than a minute and usually disappears just as fast. In the worst cases, a brain freeze keeps driving stabbing pains in a person's head for as long as five minutes. No one knows with certainty what neural mechanisms lie behind a brain freeze, but a few research findings can be helpful in preventing it. If you want to give yourself brain freeze, gulp down a big bite of ice cream so it presses against the rear part of the roof of your mouth—the most likely trigger for brain freeze. If you don't want an ice-cream headache, take a doctor's best advice: Eat slowly!

shown as being in movies and magic shows, this research shows that the brain can influence the perception of pain.

Personal experience also shows that some people can tolerate more pain than others. Some people whine over a stubbed toe, and others seem as if they could shake off a sledgehammer blow to the head. To some extent, that tolerance comes from the pain threshold—how much of an injuring stimulus it takes to feel pain. Studies show that females feel pain at a lower stimulus intensity than do males. The difference, though, tends to be small. Likewise, individual differences probably make more of an impact. In the long run, the cause of a difference between the sexes could come more from culture than from the cortex. For example, men may be taught to not mention their pain. Nevertheless, there are of course males who wince at the most minor injury, and females who rarely show outward signs of pain.

As with other forms of sensation and perception, touch—from identifying an object to feeling the wind blow across your skin to noticing temperature and experiencing pain—gathers up information from a wide range of nervous system resources. Although something external might turn on just one of a person's touch-sensitive receptors, an entire arsenal of decoding equipment comes into play as he or she attempts to turn that into a perception.

■ **Learn more about the contents of this chapter** Search the Internet for *somatosensory cortex*, *pain tolerance*, and *touch acuity*.

8 | Proprioception

In 1977, a 27-year-old woman—in seemingly excellent health—started dropping things. She also started to wobble on her feet. As time passed, the symptoms grew worse until, eventually, she couldn't even stand up. She couldn't keep her hands in one place without watching them, visually forcing them to stay put. Worse still, her jaw dropped open and she couldn't keep her mouth closed. As Oliver Sacks reported in *The Man Who Mistook His Wife for a Hat*, she said, "I can't feel my body."[12]

People don't think much about feeling their bodies. This sensation just seems to happen on its own, mostly unconsciously. If you think about it, though, you know right where your hands are, even if they are behind your back. In 1906, the great neurobiologist Sir Charles Sherrington called this "our secret sense; our sixth sense." Today, scientists call this **proprioception**. This word is a combination of the Latin word *proprius*—which means "one's own"—and the word *perception*. It is the sense of where your body parts are and where they are in relation to everything else. It is the sense that helps someone catch a baseball behind his back and even contributes to capabilities that many people take entirely for granted, such as walking or even just standing still.

The 27-year-old woman lost her sense of proprioception because of an infection of the nervous system called acute polyneuritis. She said, "I may 'lose' my arms. I think they're in one place, and I find they're [in] another."[13] Even after curing the infection, the woman's symptoms remained. Eventually, she relearned how to do many daily tasks, but to do this she watched her body's movements instead of feeling them.

SIXTH-SENSE RECEPTORS

The sense of proprioception comes from **proprioceptors**. These receptors exist in joints, muscles, skin, and tendons. It takes all of these to get a complete picture of the location of your body parts. The inner ear also provides information about balance and motion that contributes to proprioception. Stretching the skin gives some feedback to the proprioceptive system and joint receptors tell the angle of the joint and where and how fast it is moving. Two of proprioception's major players are **muscle spindles** and **Golgi tendon organs**.

Muscle spindles make up the most common proprioceptors. In general, these receptors keep track of the length of muscles—particularly any change in length. These receptors lie inside of a capsule that is inside a muscle. A sensory neuron wraps around the center of a muscle spindle, with the main part of the muscle spindle acting as a spring. When a muscle stretches, the muscle spindles get stretched and that turns on the sensory neuron. In general, that activity causes the muscle itself to contract. Overall, the muscles get stretched, which stretches the muscle spindles, and then that triggers signals that make the muscle contract and keep it from stretching too much. There's even a mechanism to make sure that the spindle stays active at most any length of a muscle. Imagine a muscle stretching and relaxing quickly. The spindle gets stretched and then the muscle relaxes. To prevent that muscle spindle from going completely limp, little muscles in the spindle contract as the overall muscle relaxes. That keeps the spindle tight and ready to respond to the next change in a muscle's length.

The next most common proprioceptor is the Golgi tendon organ (Figure 8.1). This receptor helps keep track of the tension on a muscle. These organs lie between a muscle and a bone and connect to fibers in the tendon. When the tendon gets stretched, so do the fibers. This turns on the Golgi tendon organ. The tension of the muscle determines how much the tendon gets stretched. The Golgi tendon organ, therefore, records that muscle tension.

As a team, the muscle spindle and Golgi tendon organ work in a chain reaction: a muscle gets stretched—maybe because a person twists into a new position—and the muscle spindles turn on. This causes the muscle to contract. The muscle pulls on its tendons, which then turn on the Golgi tendon organs. The Golgi tendon organs then keep track of how much tension gets put on the muscle.

UNDERSTANDING REFLEXES

Muscles spindles contribute to the knee-jerk reflex (Figure 8.2). When a physician takes a rubber hammer and taps just below your knee, your lower leg kicks. This results from a series of events. The hammer hits a tendon that stretches the front thigh muscle. This stretching activates muscle spindles in the thigh muscle. These receptors send out signals through axons that connect to neurons in the spinal cord. These neurons send another signal back to the thigh muscle, making it contract and extending your leg with a little jerk. At the same time, the signals turn off the muscles that oppose the action of the thigh extension, making it even easier for the leg to jerk.

It doesn't stop there. Some of the information also goes to the brain, especially the cerebellum, the part of the brain that

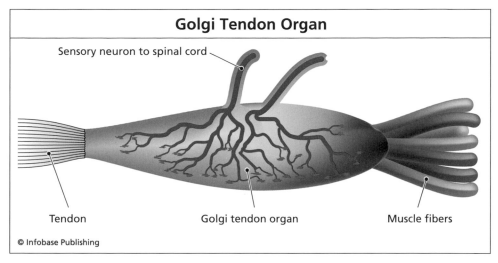

Golgi Tendon Organ

Sensory neuron to spinal cord

Tendon   Golgi tendon organ   Muscle fibers

© Infobase Publishing

Figure 8.1 Golgi tendon organs lie in tendons, which connect muscles to bones. They keep track of the tension on a muscle.

coordinates the movements of the body. It is possible to show that other parts of the nervous system can impact the knee-jerk reaction. Here's an experiment that your doctor can help you perform: Sit in a relaxed position and let your doctor tap just below your knee with a rubber-headed hammer. Have someone else try to measure how high your foot jerks. Then, grab your hands and pull them away from each other, keeping your fingers locked, as hard as you can while your doctor taps your knee again—once more recording the height of your foot's jerk. It jerks higher now. This is called the Jendrassik maneuver, a routine test in a neurological exam. Although no one knows just how it works, activating the arm muscles turns up the sensitivity of the knee-jerk reflex. Somewhere in the nervous system, the information from the arms and the knees gets combined.

Eventually, the information from muscle spindles, Golgi tendon organs, and joint receptors are combined in the brain. This collection of information gives people their sense of place in

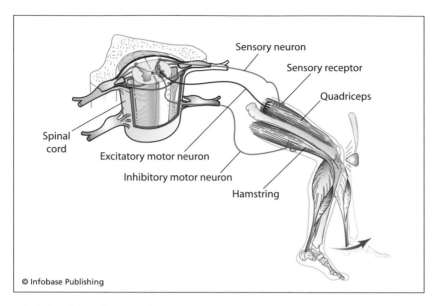

Figure 8.2 A rubber hammer's tap just below the knee sets off a chain reaction. First, the tap stretches the quadriceps at the front of the thigh, which stretches its muscle spindles. Those cells send signals to the spinal cord, which generates nerve signals that trigger contraction of the quadriceps, so that it doesn't stretch too much. Also, the hamstring is inhibited. As a result, the foot jerks forward.

space, their sense of proprioception. Scientists can use fMRI to watch some aspects of proprioception in action. For example, if someone moves a finger, part of the somatosensory cortex turns on. It apparently records the movement, or the change in location and position of the finger.

PHANTOM LIMBS

Proprioception tells a person what is where in terms of his body. In some cases, the nervous system convinces a person that something is there even when it is not. In 1866, American doctor Silas Weir Mitchell published such a scenario and called it a phantom limb. A phantom limb develops when someone has an arm or a leg amputated but still feels like the limb is there. This can develop over time after an amputation—sometimes in weeks or even in just days. Moreover, the sensation can come and go. For some people, phantom limb sensations can last for years after the amputation.

Most people who have lost a limb experience a phantom limb. It seems real to them, just as real as any limb feels to anyone else. A person who lost an arm might feel a phantom arm swinging along as usual while she walks. If someone missing his lower arm reaches for his morning coffee, he might feel phantom fingers trying to pick up the cup. The illusion goes even further: some people with phantom limbs even "feel" things on it, like a watch or ring. Perhaps worst of all, a phantom limb can hurt. It can even hurt constantly. A person with a phantom limb can feel burning, itching, scratching, and even intense shooting pain from a limb long gone. Some people even feel twisting and other sensations that a normal limb might experience.

But is it real? Scientists once thought, no—it's trauma, or maybe a desire to regain the lost limb, said some researchers. It's something generated in the mind, something fake. But is it? Ultimately, all perceptions arise from the mind through some complex interaction of neurons. Somehow, the brain keeps telling a person who is missing a limb that the limb is still there, just as it used to be—despite the lack of ordinary sensory input.

In people with phantom limbs, their somatosensory cortex keeps the mechanisms for monitoring the lost limb. Even in someone with all of their limbs, stimulating the right spot on the somatosensory cortex can result in a feeling like a limb is being touched. After amputation of the right arm, the part of the somatosensory cortex responsible for that limb does not grow dead or silent. It stays active. Moreover, following amputation, the somatosensory cortex can be rewired to some extent. That rewiring can even make a person "feel" a lost limb when other parts of the body are touched.

It can become even more complicated. A lost arm's receptive field can be rewired to the face. In fact, a complete sensory map of that arm can develop. For example, some research shows that a lost arm's hand and fingers can be "felt" by stimulating the face—seeming to the person as if his arm was just moved to a new position. Even more amazing, the new map can detect more than just touch. If a person who has lost a finger feels that lost finger when touching a spot on his chin, and then places a drop of water on that spot, he feels as if the lost finger is wet. A complete understanding of what causes a phantom limb remains to be discovered. What scientists do know, however, is that a phantom limb seems just as real as any other, at least in the brain.

Phantom Limbs in Prosthetics

Most of the time, a phantom limb seems more like a hindrance than a help. Still, it can help in one arena—prosthetics. If someone loses an arm but retains the sensation of a phantom arm, the phantom feelings can help the person learn to use the engineered artificial limb.

Moreover, phantom limbs might lead the way to even more advanced prosthetics. For example, William Craelius of Rutgers University developed an artificial hand that includes controllable fingers. The real hurdle in getting such a device to work is finding a way for the person to communicate with the machine. To do that, Craelius makes use of the phantom limb. He electrically connects the device to neurons in the arm that make the person feel like her real fingers are moving. With a little training, moving her phantom fingers makes the artificial ones move and creates a hand that is almost real.

A team of researchers at the University of Bath in the United Kingdom found that, in addition to hurting and itching, phantom limbs can also feel stiff. These scientists found amputees who had suffered from rheumatoid arthritis before losing a limb, and they experienced just as much stiffness in the phantom limb as they did in the intact one. Even more amazing, the phantom limb's stiffness responded to the same medication that eased the joints of the intact limb. Maybe the stiffness starts in the limb, but it must also change the brain. That change in the brain remains even when the joint is long gone. This shows the interaction that goes on in the nervous system for a wide range of touch sensations and perceptions.

■ **Learn more about the contents of this chapter**   Search the Internet for *proprioception*, *autonomic reflexes*, and *phantom limbs*.

9 | Synesthesia

A man experienced a bitter taste as he used his hands to form hamburger patties. A woman saw blue every time that she heard a piano ring out with a note of C. She saw different colors with different notes. In fact, when she looked at a piano's keyboard, the ivory keys looked color-coded. Another person saw printed numbers in color—a specific color for each digit. For these people,[14] one sense is perceived as another, or at least combined in some way, in a condition called **synesthesia**.

This word comes from two Greek roots: *syn*, meaning "together," and *aistesis*, meaning "perception." It simply refers to the blending of two or more senses. People with this condition—what some consider a gift—can combine any variety of senses: touch with taste, sound with color, even color vision with black and white, and on and on. The most common form is seeing letters or numbers in color—specific letters and numbers being particular colors. It can even work so that specific words appear in specific colors. To such a person, a page in a book might look like splashes of color. It seems that almost any combination of the senses can develop. Some synesthetes (people with synesthesia) feel things when they see. In fact, some people combine three or four perceptions with a single kind of sensation—such as, hearing, feeling, and smelling when they see something.

Keep in mind, too, that synesthesia develops as uniquely as people do. Among those who see colors for letters, they usually see their own unique code. One person might always see the letter *P* in blue, while that letter might look red to another synesthete. In fact, synesthetes all seem to experience their own unique world. For example, one woman felt brushing on her ankles and face when she heard guitar music. A trumpet made her feel the brushing on her back. The same woman also saw letters and numbers in color. As you might imagine, so much sensory information could be too much to handle, and some synesthetes do say that it can be completely distracting. In most cases, though, these folks seem unimpeded by the onslaught of perceptions.

DEMOGRAPHICS OF SYNESTHESIA

These mixed-up perceptions impact more people than one might imagine. Some studies indicate that only 1 person in 100,000 experiences synesthesia; other studies suggest that synesthesia could be present in 1 person in 200. Some studies even suggest that many people could be synesthetes and not even know it, although it's difficult to imagine how this joining of the senses could go unnoticed. Perhaps, a synesthete simply thinks that everyone experiences the world as a combination of perceptions, a constant explosion of sensations erupting at once.

The data indicate that there are more women than men with synesthesia. In the United States, a synesthete is three times more likely to be female. Other factors also increase the odds of being a synesthete. Left-handed people experience synesthesia more often than right-handed people, and it is more common in people of average or above-average intelligence. Also, synesthesia seems to run in families. A person's odds of experiencing a multisensational world go up if one of his or her parents is a synesthete.

THE HISTORY OF SYNESTHESIA

In 1880, synesthesia reached the scientific literature. Sir Francis Galton, a cousin of Charles Darwin (creator of modern evolutionary theory), published a paper about synesthesia. Galton's paper appeared in *Nature,* one of the world's most reputable scientific journals. For a while, synesthesia captured lots of scientific attention, but it went out of fashion among researchers by the mid-1900s. Most researchers believed that synesthesia did not arise from a twist in nervous system development. Instead, some scientists believed that synesthetes faked it. Others thought that drug use triggered the condition. In fact, drugs such as LSD and mescaline can create similar results. To many scientists, synesthesia seemed like a curiosity and not worthy of scientific investigation.

That all changed in the mid-1970s, when Larry Marks of Yale University published a review of the early synesthesia research. Following the publication of this paper, modern research into synesthesia began. The first question scientists asked was whether synesthesia is in fact real. To explore that question, one group of scientists asked synesthetes to write down the color they saw when reading 100 different words. A year later, the same subjects once more labeled the same words with colors. The results showed that these individuals labeled the words as the same colors about 90% of the time. This consistency over time made some scientists start to believe that synesthesia is real.

But even more evidence would emerge. A team of scientists used fMRI to look at the brains of synesthetes. When someone who claimed to hear in color listened to a sound, the visual areas in the brain turned on along with the auditory ones. That doesn't happen in most people. These experiments added further support to the idea that synesthesia is real.

Further evidence of the validity of synesthesia is illustrated by the following experiment. A person with synesthesia was known to see red when he saw the number 5. When researchers asked this person to add 2 and 3 in his head, he perceived red. That is, he didn't need to see the 5 to perceive red. Simply thinking of adding 2 and 3 to get 5 gave him a perception of red. So perceiving red with 5 does not rely on his eyes actually seeing it. His brain creates the connection between the number and the color.

TESTING THIS PHENOMENON

The experiments with arithmetic suggest that synesthesia takes place in the brain and is not some oddity in the sensory receptors themselves. To study this more carefully, Colin Blakemore and his colleagues at Oxford University in the United Kingdom found a group of people who claimed to hear in color, but who had lost their sight. Maybe they really had specific colors related to specific sounds, or maybe they just imagined it.

These subjects—all blind for at least 10 years—would probably not "see" the same colors with the same sounds all the time if it were just their imaginations that created the perception of color. Blakemore's team asked the subjects to say what colors they perceived when they heard the days of the week, letters, and numbers. Next, Blakemore's team waited two months, and then surprised the subjects with a second test. The results of that second test—set up just like the first one—gave startlingly similar results. Blakemore reported that someone who in the first test said hearing the letter *A* created a pale-green perception called it light or pale green in the second test. Apparently, the sensation is real, or else the subjects happen to be extremely good at remembering which colors they associated with various sounds in the first test. In an odd twist, two of the subjects in

Blakemore's group claimed to see colors as they read Braille, a system of raised dots on a page that correspond to letters in the alphabet, allowing blind people to read with their fingers. Just like the other synesthetes tested, those with what the scientists called colored-Braille also associated consistent colors with the same letters and numbers.

Synesthetic abilities can also be examined using a test called pop-out segregation. In this test, someone might draw straight lines all over a piece of paper—dozens of straight lines—and just a few tilted ones. The tilted ones pop out. One can see them immediately. Similarly, if only straight lines cover a piece of paper, and most of the lines are blue and a few are green, the green ones stand out. On the other hand, if one uses a computer to make rows and rows of black 5s and throw in just a couple of random 2s, the 2s are very difficult for most people to see (Figure 9.1).

But what about a synesthete who sees numbers in different colors? To them, the 2s should pop out—just like the few green lines among the blue ones. To test this idea, a scientist made a sheet of 5s and added in 2s that made a triangular shape. Then, the scientist asked subjects—some synesthetes and some not—to describe the shape that the 2s made. People without synesthesia did not see the triangle of 2s, but the synesthetes saw it about 90% of the time. A 90% hit ratio is what people without synesthesia get if the 5s are black and the 2s are printed in a color.

DIAGNOSING SYNESTHESIA
It seems like distinguishing someone who is a synesthete from someone who is not would be easy enough. Still, being sure who has synesthesia depends on some guidelines. Some scientists think that a few characteristics of the experience make the difference.

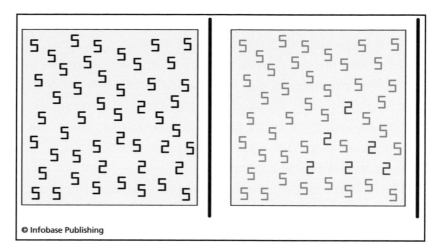

© Infobase Publishing

Figure 9.1 In the image at the left, there appears to be no pattern. If you look closely, however, you see a few 2s scattered among the 5s. For a synesthete who sees the 5s in green and the 2s in red, as shown on the right, the 2s jump out in a triangular pattern.

First, the abilities in synesthesia are automatic. Anyone can see a black 2 and imagine how it would look in red, but that takes a bit of concentration. For a synesthete, it just happens. Moreover, some synesthetes do not really see that color inside their head. Instead, it appears projected outside the body.

Synesthesia also occurs consistently. It does not just happen now and then. It happens all of the time. These perceptions also tend to be extremely memorable. If, for example, a synesthete sees the word *motorcycle* in purple, they might remember the color purple for the idea of a motorcycle before remembering the word itself.

Last, some scientists believe that a true synesthete feels an emotion along with the perception. Keep in mind, though, that synesthesia is present in a variety of forms. Therefore, the features of an individual's condition could vary as well.

PROCESSING IN SYNESTHESIA

No one knows exactly what causes synesthesia. Still, some scientists make guesses. Maybe it arises from cross-wiring in the brain. For example, in the hypothetical synesthete who sees purple when hearing the word *motorcycle*, maybe some auditory neurons connect to visual neurons, particularly where color vision takes place. This explanation appeared decades ago, but it has not been easy to confirm.

The communication between neurons arises from neurotransmitters—chemical messengers—and so it is also possible that these compounds cause the overlap between senses. For example, a neurotransmitter released from one sensory

Neurons That Respond to Vision and Touch

Sometimes, synesthesia even jumps between people in a way. Scientists at University College London found a woman who felt touch when she saw someone else being touched. In fact, if this woman saw someone else getting touched on the hand, she felt a touch in the same spot. Using fMRI, scientists compared the brains of this woman and a dozen nonsynesthetes during the perception of touch. The results showed that the somatosensory cortex turned on when any of the subjects— synesthete or not—saw someone else get touched. Moreover, if the touch was on someone else's face, the subject's face area of the somatosensory cortex showed activity. For the synesthete woman, though, the somatosensory area turned on at higher levels than in the other subjects.

Maybe everyone possesses some of the tools or connections needed for synesthesia. But the volume, so to speak, might be turned up in people who notice the combination of senses.

area of the brain could affect a different sensory area, as well. Maybe it is even more fundamental. Maybe a synesthete's brain develops differently from the brains of other people. Some scientists hypothesize that synesthetes simply have more neurons than other people. The extra neurons might lead to more connections between different sensory areas in the brain. It even appears possible that everyone starts out with a synesthete's brain, but that the sensory-mixing parts—for example, areas of the brain that combine visual and hearing information—get weeded out as an infant grows.

Many scientists would love to explore the brain of a synesthete. Although this can be done with noninvasive techniques like fMRI, there is not enough detail to see precisely what is different.

FAMOUS SYNESTHETES

This condition impacted the lives of some extremely creative people. Novelist Vladimir Nabokov saw colors with some letters—even seeing different colors with different pronunciations of the same letter in some cases. Richard Feynman—a physicist who won the Nobel Prize—experienced color with letters, too. He wrote in his autobiography, *What Do You Care What Other People Think?*, "When I see equations, I see the letters in colors—I don't know why. As I'm talking, I see vague pictures of Bessel functions. . . with light tan j's, slightly violet-bluish n's, and dark brown x's flying around."[15] It is even possible that synesthesia contributed to the creativity of those great thinkers.

■ **Learn more about the contents of this chapter** Search the Internet for *synesthete*, *synesthesia and fMRI*, and *genetics of synesthesia*.

10 | Damage and Repair

Stefan Suchert worked as an attorney in Nuremburg, Germany. One tragic day, he found out that both of his sons would likely go blind from a disease in which their eyesight would gradually grow worse over time. It seemed like an intolerable loss, especially since both of his boys were born deaf as well. Suchert quit his law practice and invested millions of dollars to start a company called Intelligent Medical Implants. His company created a retina implant. This small gold chip will eventually include a video camera that picks up light signals and then uses 49 electrodes to send the information to ganglion cells—basically bypassing a damaged retina. Although this device remains under development, implanted chips that received information from a computer allowed a few test patients to see lines, sometimes even moving lines.

VISUAL DAMAGE AND REPAIR

Many people suffer from vision problems, which often are a result of the aging process. In the United States, millions of people suffer from poor vision or blindness. For Americans over the age of 40, the most common visual diseases include **macular degeneration**, **glaucoma**, and **cataracts**. The most common problems also vary according to race. Macular degeneration causes the most blindness in Caucasian Americans, and cataracts and glaucoma cause the most trouble for African Americans. For Hispanics, glaucoma causes more blindness than the other diseases.

Macular degeneration affects about 10 million Americans and 50 million people around the world.[16] In this disease, the retina deteriorates, or gets worse over time, especially affecting central vision. This disease also has a genetic component, and scientists know several of the key genes involved. Still, macular degeneration is not just passed along through a person's genes. It tends to develop after the age of 60, and a poor diet and smoking play a role. Laser treatments can help some forms of macular degeneration, but some cases can only be repaired with an artificial retina. More than 20 such devices are under development.

So far, even the best artificial retinas provide only meager black-and-white vision that is far from sufficient for useful vision. Keep in mind, too, that scientists started this battle long ago. Even in the 1960s, Giles Brindley of the Medical Research Council in London tried implanting electrodes in a blind person's visual cortex. He wanted to completely bypass the eye, delivering the information directly to the brain.

Much of today's work, focuses on stimulating the retina itself. For example, Alan Chow's team at Optobionics in Naperville, Illinois, uses a device called a subretinal implant. This approach stimulates cells in the middle of the retina. This approach assumes that only the photoreceptors themselves are damaged, and that the rest of the retina still works.

Chow's device consists of a silicon disk that includes 5,000 photodiodes, or solar cells that generate an electrical signal when stimulated with light. This technique has reached the stage of clinical trials, which are test-runs on actual people. This is a crucial step in getting approval from the U.S. Food and Drug Administration for using this therapeutic approach. Of the 10 people in the first clinical trial, all experienced some improvement in vision, although it was sometimes only an increased sensitivity to light. Sometimes, though, Chow's technique provided even more improvement. For instance, after receiving the implant, a woman who was legally blind could see enough to thread a needle.

Different techniques are used to treat glaucoma. In glaucoma, a person suffers from increased pressure inside the eye. Eventually, the higher pressure can damage cells and create blindness. In a normal eye, fluid flows in and out of a space near the front of the eye and removes waste and provides nutrients to the lens and cornea. In an eye affected by glaucoma, the fluid goes in faster than it goes out. In some cases, glaucoma can be treated with medication, such as eyedrops; other cases require surgery to relieve the pressure.

With cataracts, the eye's lens becomes cloudy and vision grows blurry and dim. This clouding develops when some of the proteins in the lens gather in clumps. This might just come with age, but researchers suspect that other factors—such as diabetes and smoking—can contribute to the problem. A cataract can develop as early as 40 years of age but tends to be more of a problem for people who are 60 or older. This can be repaired surgically, by replacing the damaged lens with a plastic one.

HEARING DAMAGE

Everyone loses some auditory ability with age. In particular, the ability to hear higher frequencies reduces as we age. By the age of 85, about half of all people suffer from notable hearing loss. Such loss can come from ordinary wear and tear or from the environment, such as too much exposure to loud noises. Hearing loss comes in two general forms: conductive hearing loss and sensorineural hearing loss (Figure 10.1). Mixed hearing loss is a combination of conductive and sensorineural hearing loss.

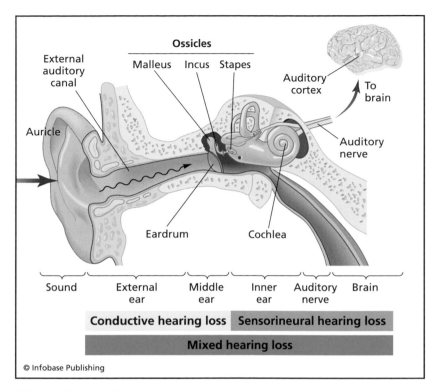

Figure 10.1 Audiologists classify hearing loss in three forms: conductive hearing loss, sensorineural hearing loss, and mixed hearing loss. Conductive hearing loss impacts the outer or middle ear. Sensorineural hearing loss comes from damage to the inner ear or the auditory pathways in the brain. Mixed hearing loss can come from all these areas.

In conductive hearing loss, sound is not carried properly from outside the ear to the cochlea. A variety of problems, even including too much wax in the outer ear, can cause conductive hearing loss. Damage to the eardrum and problems with the bones of the middle ear—the malleus, incus, and stapes—can also create conductive hearing loss. These problems reduce the sensitivity of hearing, making it difficult to hear softer sounds. In most cases, though, conductive hearing loss can be treated. For example, a hearing aid can be inserted in the ear to increase the volume of sounds.

Sensorineural hearing loss comes from problems with the cochlea or the auditory nerves that carry information from the cochlea to the brain. Historically, this condition could not be treated, and problems with sensitivity and understanding speech can arise. Many events, such as disease, some drugs, and loud noises can cause sensorineural hearing loss. As with conductive hearing loss, sensorineural hearing loss can come with age.

REPAIRING HEARING LOSS

If hearing damage occurs in the cochlea, an electronic device called an artificial cochlea or a cochlear implant can sometimes be used as a treatment. These implants consist of external and internal parts. The external parts, a microphone and speech processor, are about as big as a deck of cards and run on a couple of batteries. The microphone picks up sounds that get refined by the speech processor and then sent to an internal receiver that is implanted surgically just behind the ear. The receiver sends electrical signals to an electrode that activates the auditory nerve. This system goes around the cochlea, taking sounds from the outside and delivering them—converted into an electrical code—to the nerve that leads to auditory areas in the brain.

An even more advanced era of auditory repair lies ahead, through what are called MEMS, or microelectromechanical systems. Scientists at the University of Michigan are developing a mechanical cochlea. This will be made from a combination of small mechanical and electronic parts. Lower cost provides a significant benefit of this approach, because micromachining allows for large production runs at relatively low costs. Right now, this device can pick up sounds. The researchers even tuned this device to focus on frequencies that mimic human hearing. The parts operate in a fluid-filled environment, just like a real cochlea. Next, the scientists must make this device send out signals that can properly turn on the auditory nerve.

AGING AND THE CORTEX

In general, a person's body wears out with age. How fast that happens varies from person to person. It surely depends on both hereditary and environmental factors. The better care someone takes of his or her body, the longer it will last, and the longer it will perform at a higher level. The ticking of the biological clock, though, cannot be stopped. Even if all the sensory organs remained operable, a person's sensory and perceptual capabilities would dwindle over the years. Part of the problem arises in the brain itself.

As one example, older people tend to be slower at sensorimotor tasks than younger people. This can be studied by looking at activity in the brain while someone works at a task; for example, responding to a visual or auditory stimulus. In one set of experiments, researchers found that older people (about 60 years old) responded slower than young ones (about 20 years old) when they had to make a movement related to some sensory cue. By recording from the brain during these actions, the scientists found that the sensory system responded about the same in both groups, but the motor system—the parts of the nervous system that control movement—was slower with age. Moreover, when the scientists tested the subjects with more complicated tasks, the difference in speed increased between the older and younger subjects. So, if nothing else, aging slows down some of the last steps in the perceptual process—especially the action.

Still, perception itself can diminish with age. At the Karolinska Institute in Stockholm, Sweden, scientists tested people of different ages for their ability to recognize facial expressions. The scientists recorded brain activity with fMRI while showing the subjects a selection of angry and neutral faces. In both older and younger subjects, this task turned on the brain, as one would expect, but it turned on different places in the brain—or at least turned on different brain areas at different levels. In the younger subjects, the faces turned on areas deeper inside the brain, whereas more cortical areas turned on when older subjects examined the faces. No one knows just what this means, except that the recognition of emotion in facial expressions differed in the subjects studied in this research, and it differed in ways that showed an age-related change. The scientists suggested that the change could arise from the cortex trying to compensate for weakening deep-brain functions as the subjects aged. On the other hand, maybe people just process emotional

Can Losing One Sensory Capability Enhance Others?

Many people have heard that blind people can compensate for the loss of sight by improving other sensory capabilities. Geerat J. Vermeij's ability to recognize shells just by feeling them provides an impressive example of this. In science, though, things that people "know" often turn out to be wrong. The only way to determine if blind people really develop better capabilities in other senses is to test this hypothesis.

At Duquesne University in Pittsburgh, Pennsylvania, Daniel Goldreich and his colleagues tested this idea. They selected people between the ages of 18 and 70 years old—some who could and others who could not see—and tested their abilities to recognize touch. An experimental system tapped a subject's finger with different pieces of plastic, which was smooth in some cases and grooved in others. The size of the grooves varied to give a range of stimuli. Then, Goldreich's team asked the subjects to say if the touch came from smooth or grooved plastic.

information—even interpreting the expression on someone's face—differently as the years pass.

In any case, scientists do know that the brain slows down in some ways with age. When it comes to perceiving sounds, the brain responds more slowly with age. If scientists make people listen to sounds and record the time from the start of the sound until auditory areas in the brain turn on, that time gets longer as the person gets older. Similar experiments with visual stimuli also show a slowing in perception with age. The years—like it or not—put wear and tear on the entire machine that runs

The scientists tapped the subject's finger with plastic with various width grooves to see how fine the grooves could be and still be distinguished from smooth. Overall, the blind subjects could detect finer grooves than the sighted people could. Not surprisingly, younger people could detect finer grooves than older people—another example of the systems weakening over the years.

You might think that blind people can sense touch better because they learn this through practice from reading Braille. Not so. Of the blind people in this study, the ones who could read Braille did not have any better sense of touch than those who couldn't read Braille. For some reason, blindness leads to better touch capabilities, but it's apparently not just from practice. In fact, of the subjects in Goldreich's research, people who were born blind did not have any better sense of touch than people who became blind at an older age. Something in the brain changes with blindness, but scientists do not know just what that is.

perceptual processing. How people take care of themselves plays a major role in how well the sensory and perceptual systems work over time.

PUTTING TOGETHER THE PIECES

In taking an overview of the research on sensation and perception, it becomes clear that scientists keep learning more and more about these processes. Some of the advances come from studying the natural history of sensation and perception, and perhaps finding people with unusual capabilities, such as synesthesia. In addition, people who suffer tragic events, such as losing a limb, can teach scientists more about how the brain processes sensory information.

As with much of science, the field of sensation and perception also advances with new technologies. For example, fMRI lets scientists watch the brain as a person processes a sight or a sound—a technological ability that was unimaginable 50 years ago. No doubt, future technologies will push this field even farther ahead. Future generations of scientists will dig even deeper into how humans and animals interpret the world in which they live.

■ **Learn more about the contents of this chapter** Search the Internet for *blindness*, *sensory prosthetics*, and *aging and perception*.

Notes

1. J.A. Hoffer, G.E. Loeb, and C.A. Pratt, "Single unit conduction velocities from averaged nerve cuff electrode records in freely moving cats," *Journal of Neuroscience Methods* 4 (1981): 211–225.

2. N. Brunel and X.J. Wang, "What determines the frequency of fast network oscillations with irregular neural discharges? I. Synaptic dynamics and excitation-inhibition balance," *Journal of Neurophysiology* 90 (2003): 415–430.

3. Robert W. Williams and Karl Herrup. "The control of neuron number," *Neurogenetics Online*, September 28, 2001, http://www.nervenet.org/papers/NUMBER_REV_1988.html#1 (accessed November 27, 2006).

4. Wallace L.M. Alward, "A new angle on ocular development," *Science* 299 (2003): 1527–1528.

5. R. Fox, S.W. Lehmluhle, and D.H. Westendorf, "Falcon visual acuity," *Science* 192 (1976): 263–265.

6. Steven Yantis. "To see is to attend," *Science* 299 (2003): 54–56.

7. A. Terry Bahill, David G. Baldwin, and Jayendran Venkateswaran. "Predicting a baseball's path," *American Scientist* 93 (2005): 218–225.

8. Eric Chudler, "The Nose Knows," *Neuroscience for Kids*, http:// faculty.washington.edu/chudler/ nosek.html (accessed November 27, 2006).

9. E. Bruce Goldstein, *Sensation and Perception*, (Pacific Grove, Calif.: Wadsworth, 2002), 481.

10. National Geographic, "Dogs in Training to Sniff Out Cancer," *National Geographic News*, August 20, 2004, http://news. nationalgeographic.com/ news/2004/08/0820_040820_ detectordogs.html.

11. Auckland Bioengineering Institute. "Special Sense Organs— Cells," *IUPS Physiome Project*, http://www.bioeng.auckland. ac.nz/physiome/ontologies/ special_sense_organs/cells.php (accessed November 27, 2006).

12. Oliver Sacks, *The Man Who Mistook His Wife for a Hat* (New York: Harper Perennial, 1970), 45.

13. Ibid., 47.

14. Vilayanur S. Ramachandran and Edward M. Hubbard, "Hearing colors, tasting shapes," *Scientific American* 288 (2003): 53–59.

15. Richard Feynman, *What Do You Care What Other People Think?* (New York: Norton, 1988), 59.

16. Jean Marx, "A clearer view of macular degeneration," *Science* 311 (2006): 1704–1705.

Glossary

Action potential A wave of electrical excitation that triggers the release of chemical messengers from nerves.

Axon Long, thin projection that transmits information away from the cell body.

Cataract Clouding of the eye's lens.

Categorical perception Dividing a range of inputs—say, every shade from white to black—into a couple of defined shades, like just black and just white.

Cerebral cortex The outer layer of neurons in the brain, which typically control more advanced functions, such as sensory processing and thinking.

Cochlea A snail shell–shaped structure inside the ear that responds to sounds of different frequencies.

Cones Cells at the back of the eye that respond to the color of light.

Cornea The clear surface that covers the front of the eye.

Dendrites Projections from the cell body of a neuron that take information to the cell body.

Dermis The lower layer of the skin.

Electromagnetic spectrum The complete range of waves that travel in space—from radio waves through gamma rays.

Epidermis The outer layer of the skin.

Eye The organ that gathers light for sight.

Frequency The numbers of waves that pass a point in a specified period of time.

Frontal cortex The front part of the brain that participates in abstract thought, movement, and other behaviors.

Functional magnetic resonance imaging (fMRI) A scanning technique that compares changes in the brain, such as blood flow, with behaviors, such as seeing or movements.

Ganglion cells Cells at the back of the eye that carry visual information to the brain.

Glaucoma Increased pressure inside the eye, which can damage vision.

Golgi tendon organs Structures that connect muscle to bone and record the tension in the muscles.

Haptic perception Feeling objects to recognize them.

Homunculus A map of the body surface in the part of the brain that records touch.

Hypothalamus A structure inside the brain that regulates survival functions, such as appetite and body temperature.

Incus A bone inside the ear that helps transmit sound from outside to inside.

Ion channels Microscopic openings in nerve cells that allow specific charged atoms to move inside cells.

Ions Charged atoms.

Lateral geniculate nucleus The first area in the brain that processes vision.

Lateral inhibition A signal from one nerve cell that prevents nearby cells from turning on.

Lens A round structure, roughly in the center of the eye, that helps focus images onto vision cells at the back of the eye.

Macula An area at the back of the eye that picks out fine details.

Macular degeneration Deterioration of the area at the back of the eye that picks out fine details.

Malleus A bone inside the ear that helps transmit sound from outside to inside.

Mechanoreceptors Nerve cells that respond to mechanical forces on structures, including the skin.

Meissner corpuscles Nerve cells that respond to ripples of touch on the skin.

Merkel receptors Nerve cells that respond to pressure on the skin.

Muscle spindles Small structures that respond to changes in length in the cells that contract to move bones.

Myelin A fatty covering that insulates some nerves and increases the speed of electrical signals moving through them.

Nanometer One-millionth of a meter.

Nerve terminals Small protrusions from the end of a nerve cell that release chemical messengers to other nerves.

Neurons Nerve cells.

Neurotransmitters Chemicals that carry messages between neurons.

Nociceptors Nerve cells that respond to pain.

Occipital cortex The back of the brain, which participates in vision.

Olfactory bulb A structure at the bottom of the brain that receives information about smell.

Olfactory epithelium A structure in the nose that receives information about smell.

Optic disk A spot in the retina where nerves carry visual information toward the brain.

Pacinian corpuscles Nerve cells that respond to vibrations on the skin.

Parietal cortex The upper-middle portion of the brain that collects and processes information from many senses.

Perception The process of gathering, interpreting, and organizing information from the senses.

Phonemes The smallest unit of sound that makes up words.

Photon The smallest particle of light.

Photopigment A molecule in the back of the eye that responds to light.

Proprioception Sensing the position of body parts in space and the movement of muscles and joints.

Proprioceptors Cells that sense the position of body parts in space and the movement of muscles and joints.

Receptive field The area where a stimulus turns on a sensory cell.

Receptors Nerve cells that respond to sensory input, such as light or sound.

Retina A thin sheet of tissue at the back of the eye that contains nerve cells that respond to light.

Retinotopic map An area of brain tissue that replicates the organization of visual stimuli that land on the back of the eye.

Rods Nerve cells in the back of the eye that respond to low levels of light, essentially "seeing" it in black and white.

Ruffini cylinders Nerve cells that respond to stretching of the skin.

Sensation An impression gained from a stimulus to nerve cells that pick up information from the environment.

Soma The cell body of a neuron.

Somatosensory cortex The part of the outer brain that gathers and processes information from the bones, joints, muscles, skin, and tendons.

Sound Vibrations picked up by the ears.

Stapes A bone inside the ear that helps transmit sound from outside to inside.

Synapse The place where neurons connect.

Synesthesia Perceiving more than one sense in combination.

Thalamus A sensory-relay station located near the base of the brain.

Taste buds Collections of nerve cells on the tongue and inside of the mouth that respond to chemicals.

Temporal cortex The part of the brain more or less behind the ear that participates in hearing and memory.

Thermoreceptors Nerve cells that respond to changes in temperature.

Tonotopic map A structure, such as part of the cochlea or an area of the brain, where different frequencies of sound activate neurons in different areas, all arranged in some order from low to high frequencies.

Transduction Changing one sort of stimulus—say, light—into a different form of information, such as the electrical and chemical signals used in the nervous system.

Tympanic membrane The eardrum, or the sheet of tissue that vibrates to transfer sound information to the inner ear.

Visual acuity The clarity of vision.

Visual cortex The rear part of the brain that gathers and processes visual information from the eyes and other parts of the brain.

Wavelength The length of a vibration from one peak or trough to the next.

Bibliography

Alward, Wallace L.M. "A new angle on ocular development." *Science* 299 (2003): 1527–1528.

Axel, Richard. "The molecular logic of smell." *Scientific American* 273 (1995): 154–159.

Botvinick, Matthew. "Probing the neural basis of body ownership." *Science* 305 (2004): 782–783.

Goldstein, E. Bruce. *Sensation and Perception.* Pacific Grove, Calif.: Wadsworth, 2002.

Gould, James, L., William T. Keeton, and Carol Grant Gould. *Biological Science.* New York: W.W. Norton & Company, 1997.

Howard Hughes Medical Institute. "Seeing, Hearing, and Smelling the World." Available online. URL: http://www.hhmi.org/senses. Accessed November 27, 2006.

Kandel, Eric R., James H. Schwartz, and Thomas M. Jessell. *Principles of Neural Science.* New York: McGraw-Hill Medical, 2000.

Logothetis, Nikos K. "Vision: a window of consciousness." *Scientific American* 281 (1999): 69–75.

Massaro, Dominic W., and David G. Stork. "Speech recognition and sensory integration." *American Scientist* 86 (1998): 236–244.

Shepherd, Gordon M. *The Synaptic Organization of the Brain.* Oxford, U.K.: Oxford University Press, 2003.

Wolfe, Jeremy M., Keith R. Kluender, Dennis M. Levi, Linda M. Bartoshuk, and Rachel S. Herz. *Sensation and Perception.* Sunderland, Mass.: Sinauer Associates Incorporated, 2005.

Yantis, Steven. "To see is to attend," *Science* 299 (2003): 54–56.

Zou, Zhihua, and Linda B. Buck. "Combinatorial effects of odorant mixes in olfactory cortex," *Science* 301 (2006): 1477–1481.

Further Reading

Ackerman, Diane. *A Natural History of the Senses*. London: Vintage, 1991.

Bahill, A. Terry, David G. Baldwin, and Jayendran Venkateswaran. "Predicting a baseball's path." *American Scientist* 93 (2005): 218–225.

Kolb, Helga. "How the retina works." *American Scientist* 91 (2003): 28–35.

Ramachandran, Vilayanur S., and Edward M. Hubbard. "Hearing colors, tasting shapes." *Scientific American* 288 (2003): 53–59.

Sacks, Oliver. *The Man Who Mistook His Wife for a Hat*. New York: Harper Perennial, 1970.

Smith, David V., and Robert F. Margolskee. "Making sense of taste." *Scientific American* 284 (2001): 32–39.

Society for Neuroscience. "Brain Facts." Available online. URL: http://www.sfn.org/index.cfm?pagename=brainFacts. Accessed November 27, 2006.

Wyttenbach, Robert A. *PsyCog: Explorations in Perception and Cognition*. Sunderland, Mass.: Sinauer Associates, 2006.

Web Sites

ePsych
> *http://epsych.msstate.edu*
> Users can read background on many topics in neurobiology. In addition, this site provides working demonstrations of many phenomena, such as the McGurk effect and motion parallax.

Exploratorium Online Exhibits
> *http://www.exploratorium.edu/exhibits/f_exhibits.html*
> This museum of science provides 13 visual illusions. This site includes movies and explanations of many perceptions.

Health Information
> *http://www.nidcd.nih.gov/health/smelltaste/*
> The U.S. National Institute on Deafness and Other Communication Disorders runs this site. It provides background on a variety of disorders related to balance, hearing, smell, and taste.

Illusions Gallery
> *http://dragon.uml.edu/psych/illusion.html*
> A collection of visual illusions—such as oddities of perceiving color and shape—help users understand the difference between reality and perception. Many of the illusions also include explanations of the perception.

Let's Play Jeopardy!
> *http://www.uni.edu/walsh/jeopardy.html*
> Test your sensation and perception knowledge by following the television game show format.

Neuroscience for Kids
> *http://faculty.washington.edu/chudler/neurok.html*
> Not just for kids, this site covers a wide range of topics in neuroscience. It includes many easy experiments and a newsletter with updates on research.

Sense of Smell Institute
> *http://www.senseofsmell.org*
> Olfaction grabs center stage on this site. It includes a virtual library of information and an olfaction glossary.

The Synesthesia Battery
http://www.synesthete.org
Here, users can assess their perceptions with a variety of tests to see if they might have synesthesia.

UCSC (University of California, Santa Cruz) Perceptual Science Lab
http://mambo.ucsc.edu
This online lab lets users explore a wide range of experimental and theoretical aspects of perception, with special emphasis on speech perception. It includes a few demonstrations and movies.

Picture Credits

All illustrations © Infobase Publishing

Index

About the Author

Mike May is a freelance science and technology writer and editor. Showing an early interest in science, May won the Bausch and Lomb Medal of Science as a high school senior in 1978. His career in science really started at Earlham College, where he earned a B.A. in biology in 1982. Next, he earned an M.S. in biological engineering from the University of Connecticut in 1984. At Connecticut, May explored the application of computer science, electrical engineering, and mathematics to neurobiology and worked in a tissue-culture laboratory. In the late 1980s, supported by a National Institutes of Health fellowship in cellular biology, he studied auditory perception in several organisms at Cornell University. In part, this work put May on a team that was the first to show categorical perception in an invertebrate, the Australian field cricket. In 1990, he earned his Ph.D. in neurobiology and behavior from Cornell. He then enjoyed seven years as an associate editor at *American Scientist* magazine, and has worked freelance since 1998. In 1999, he won a THOR Center for Neuroinformatics Citation for writing "VRML for Biology," which appeared on Elsevier's H.M.S. *Beagle* Web site.

About the Editor

Eric H. Chudler, Ph.D., is a research neuroscientist who has investigated the brain mechanisms of pain and nociception since 1978. Dr. Chudler received his Ph.D. from the Department of Psychology at the University of Washington in Seattle. He has worked at the National Institutes of Health and directed a laboratory in the neurosurgery department at Massachusetts General Hospital. Between 1991 and 2006, Dr. Chudler was a faculty member in the Department of Anesthesiology at the University of Washington. He is currently a research associate professor in the University of Washington Department of Bioengineering and director of education and outreach at University of Washington Engineered Biomaterials. Dr. Chudler's research interests focus on how areas of the central nervous system (cerebral cortex and basal ganglia) process information related to pain. He has also worked with other neuroscientists and teachers to develop educational materials to help students learn about the brain.